Advance Praise for
Across The Kitchen Table

"My wife and I first met Pam in the early '90s in a Minneapolis church pew attending our first home-school conference. Pam didn't know our situation from anyone's, but her warmth and understanding attracted our attention. She also didn't know it, but I was a public school teacher attending the conference on behalf of my wife who was softening up to this 'strange' home-school movement.

"Pam helped break the prejudice I had—along with many professionals in the public and parochial school systems—that home educators were merely delinquents. *Across the Kitchen Table* brings the revolution of home education into your home with the same grandmotherly, 'babushka' spirit that greeted us ten years ago.

"Pam's memoirs remind us of what an adventure home education is. *Across the Kitchen Table* brings us through her early years as a home-school pioneer, rummaging for phonics programs and being an outlaw under a superintendent who vowed to defeat the homeschoolers in her district. She reminds all home-school parents of the freedoms we enjoy today.

"Wendy and I love Pam von Gohren."

Chris Jeub, Web editor to Parents' Place, Focus on the Family

"A must read for all homeschooling parents! Full of practical tools, insightful ideas, encouraging words, and convicting wisdom from a veteran homeschooling mother, now grandma, who successfully mentored four children into adulthood and is now guiding the next generation. Granny's (Her) vignettes cover a wide variety of topics and can easily be used for daily inspiration for homeschooling parent/teachers, support groups, or anyone interested in educating children."

> *Valerie Swedlund, B.S., former teacher, educational consultant, and learning styles specialist*

"Every home-school family will benefit from the practical, insightful thoughts in *Across the Kitchen Table*. After reading your book I am again encouraged to simply talk informally with our own children about life issues. It is too easy to reduce homeschooling to 'getting through the curriculum.' I pray that your book will redirect families back to meaningful conversation with their children around the kitchen table."

> *David Quine, Cornerstone Curriculum Project*

Across the
KITCHEN TABLE

Across the
KITCHEN TABLE

Pamela Read von Gohren

Beaver's Pond Press, Inc.

Edina, *Minnesota*

Bible quotations are from New International Version unless otherwise noted.

ISBN 1-931646-32-5

Library of Congress Catalog Number: 2002103919

Cover and Interior Design by Mori Studio

Printed in the United States of America

First Printing: April 2002

06 05 04 03 02   6 5 4 3 2 1

Beaver's Pond Press, Inc.

5125 Danen's Drive
Edina, MN 55439-1465
(952) 829-8818
www.beaverspondpress.com

to order, visit Learning at Home Successfully
www.isd.net/home-ed-pro.

Blest be this house...
and all who dwell
within.

LSR 1986

Dedication

To Jerry, the Big Kids, and the Little Boys.

Table of Contents

Foreword

Few families have homeschooled longer than our family (we began in 1981), but the von Gohrens have us beat. The very first time I met Pam von Gohren I knew that she was someone special. The thing that impressed me was she knew the Minnesota home school law better than I did, and I was the attorney assigned by Home School Legal Defense Association to protect our member families in that state.

That began a long relationship with Pam as we worked together to protect the freedoms the homeschoolers had earned in Minnesota. She was instrumental in keeping the legislature from eroding the freedom granted home scholars in Minnesota.

Pam is uniquely qualified to give advice regarding homeschooling. The proof is in the pudding as it relates to her success in teaching her children at home. All of her children are grown and reflect the extraordinary parenting skills of Jerry and Pam.

There are many resources available to homeschoolers out there today, but *Across the Kitchen Table* is a must for any mom who has a desire to improve relationships with her children and husband, and have fun while doing it. The insights that Pam shares in this book are unique in that they come from a mom who has not only actually homeschooled, but because of the age of her children, has had an opportunity to examine whether her techniques were effective.

Pam's unique writing style, wisdom, and humor, also makes *Across the Kitchen Table* a must for any mom who needs a little encouragement regarding the wisdom of choosing home education as the method for discipling her family.

J. Michael Smith, president,
Home School Legal Defense Association

ACKNOWLEDGEMENTS

I didn't start out to write a book, but the good people identified below made sure one got published. Ruth L. sparked the idea of the newsletter column, "Granny's Observations" from which these essays grew. Connie D. (and other gracious home-educating parents) encouraged me to keep writing those observations. Cathi and Jan, plus the other Cyber-Space Angels interceded long and often that I might complete the task, especially the rewriting chores. Emily and Lud proofread, critiqued, and massaged my hunched-over-the-computer shoulders.

My mom, Lori Read, created the counted cross-stitch house blessing that appears above the Dedication and on the chapter title pages. And, my dad, Walter, reminded me in overwhelmed moments that "of course, you can complete this." I love them both for instilling in me the courage to give things a try.

Finally, the wonderful folks at Beaver's Pond Press and Mori Studio pulled everything together, making the publishing process an enjoyable adventure.

Everyone of you is a blessing and much appreciated.

INTRODUCTION

A few years ago, I was asked to begin writing a regular column for the publication, Paper Mache, *the bimonthly newsletter of the Minnesota Association of Christian Home Educators. The mission statement was straightforward: provide reassurance, share teaching tips, and offer insight and hindsight accumulated from my (then) nearly twenty years of home-educating experience. "Could you sprinkle it with a bit of humor, too?" the editor requested. This book is based on those articles, originally titled "Granny's Observations."*

The short essays that comprise this volume are meant to bolster a mom who needs some quick sustenance—especially before facing her recess-refreshed horde invigorated by the backyard playground. Moms need recess too. Yet what rejuvenates them is mental and emotional fortification as much as physical activity. I'm told many of the original "Granny's" are kept in the bathroom for hurried perusal.

My husband and I taught and parented without benefit of nearby relatives. Half a continent separates us from our folks and the grandparents, aunts, uncles, and cousins. There were so many moments when I desperately wanted a hug and a reassuring pat to restore my courage to return to the fray of raising adults from the mire of childishness. Long-distance telephone calls were a tremendous blessing. Though physical touch was missing, warm, caring voices came across the miles to bolster me for another hour or week.

Sitting before my computer, column on deadline, I envision the moms and dads who've telephoned or come to our home over the years to talk about how to teach their kids. Despite earnest hopes and sound intentions, in the press of day-to-day, their dream bubble bursts. Home education is neither easy nor a quick fix and it is an awesome consumer of energy. My husband and I pour a cup of tea or coffee for visitors, pray together, and simply converse. Remembering a discussion during which my visiting mother exclaimed, "Of course, you are feeling overwhelmed; you're in your busy years!" we don't propose profound solutions, but we surely do empathize.

You will notice that I do not use our children's names when writing about their exploits. This is deliberate. During their growing-up years, our kids endured numerous interviews with reporters and legislators as well as the ongoing scrutiny of people curious to see how home-educated children would turn out. They've earned the right to anonymity, especially now that they are raising their own families.

This book is written mom-to-mom. These are the stories you would hear while drinking tea at my kitchen table. Maybe you need your spine restarched or a chuckle or a new slant on a situation. These pages extend "been-there, lived-through-that" reassurance for your adventure. May it be a satisfying one that you will treasure in your memories!

Pam "Granny" von Gohren
Minnetonka, Minnesota

1

Philosophy

Pioneer Remembrances
Granny
The Beginning
Where Are We Going?

PIONEER REMEMBRANCES

"Superintendent drill, Mom" our son hissed urgently. Sure enough, the unique whine of a local official's automobile transmission was audible a block away. Quickly the children gathered up books and moved to the walkout level of our home beyond sight of a visitor. Although we had home-educated for six-and-a-half years without problems, the assistant superintendent of schools had recently vowed to turn in to the county attorney, on charges of neglect and abuse, anyone found to be teaching their children at home. Thus far three families had been affected.

This was 1984 when nonpublic schools in our state were to be essentially equivalent to the government schools. Our friends were accused of noncompliance because their bookshelves held fewer volumes than those at the local elementary school: no matter that they carried home stacks of books every week from the regional library. We felt particularly vulnerable because my husband, Jerry, served on a blue ribbon district committee chaired by the same assistant superintendent who frequently dropped reports off at our home. Blessedly, we remained hidden, all the while walking a fine line to teach the children appropriate respect for authority though quietly practicing what some would allege to be civil disobedience.

Often we took our family vacation in September, enjoying nice weather but minimal crowds after government schools commenced. A 1985 trip to the East Coast focused on American history. Picking up passes at our congressman's office to venues in Washington, D.C., we were suddenly surrounded by his entire staff after one of the children admitted to school being located at the kitchen table. Moving in pairs, his legislative assistants interviewed each one of our children individually as well as Jerry and myself. "Thank you for answering our questions," the legislative director remarked, "we know that home educators exist, but, until now, we hadn't had personal contact with any. Your children are wonderful! Do home educators need any special legislation or protections?"

Our community support group organized in 1982–83 with four families; then we grew slowly to twenty-five households. This turned out to be a size that permitted knowing each other well, provided sufficient numbers to keep organizational tasks "parent-sized," and enough children for playmates and friendships. When home education in Minnesota became clearly legal in August 1987, we were inundated with two hundred membership requests. Feverishly we sorted people into age or geographical groupings, passed out the lists, and blessed the new educators' (anticipated) success. The experience proved that coordinators do emerge when needed. Our paramount advice to new leadership was that loving and assisting each other is much more important than providing calendars full of programs and activities.

One day our group went on a field trip to Pike Island Nature Center, located at Fort Snelling State Park. Inside the grounds, there seemed to be more ranger vehicles than normal along the roadway. We chalked it up to a sunny day encouraging extra visitors. The nature center staff, however, was tense, casting furtive, then puzzled, looks at the moms and children trooping into the gathering area. "Minnetonka Home Education Association is ready to begin," I beamed at the receptionist. "W-who are you?" she stammered, explaining that they had thought the reservation was for the county home school, a residential facility for male juvenile delinquents, also located in Minnetonka.

Finding teaching materials was a struggle "way back when." Neither secular nor Christian publishers knowingly sold to parent-educators. "Get those kids back into school where they belong," was the emphatic message. We had some success soliciting "preview texts" for our "curriculum selection committee" via letterhead that was pompously official: Hunter Academy, Gerald L. von Gohren, Headmaster, address, phone, and fax. Mostly we visited Goodwill and Salvation Army used book rooms on each trip downtown. "Lord, you know our present and future needs. Please lead us to what will be useful," we murmured. The treasures He provided boggled our minds in their specificity, quality, and quantity. Conference exhibit halls are wonderful, but today's parents, shopping for materials, miss our spiritual adventures.

During legislative skirmishes, the children tagged along, completing assignments as debate droned. Later, earning Boy Scout merit badges motivated a formal civics unit study and organized those Capitol Building memories. We discovered that school board candidates welcomed people of all ages as campaign participants. Our brood was included in backroom strategy sessions as well as in the more typical tasks of envelope stuffing and pounding yard signs. By their mid-teens, when we petitioned for equal access to high school extracurricular activities, our crew had elected a majority of the school board—which then passed our request unanimously.

At 10 A.M. one September morning, we lined up at a sports equipment retailer's giant tent sale on the prowl for cross-country ski boots. The salesman challenged the boys looking for bargains during school hours. Their assurance that they were officially released for shopping didn't satisfy this gentleman who, it turned out, had been a senior high school teacher. "Never heard of it," he glared suspiciously when they named their institution. "Guess you didn't watch Channel 4 TV last night," the boys smiled. "Ours was the featured school in the education segment!" Another skeptic became enlightened.

The WCCO-TV reporters had by then become friends, although the first visit was a white-knuckle affair. Not knowing what or where they would film, we cleaned everything— except the workshop where our nine-year-old son had built a wind tunnel to verify the aerodynamics of his model car designs. Mercifully the cameraman put the background into very soft focus.

All our children have graduated. They are scattered across the country and the globe. Assembled for a family reunion, they reminisced about their days at Hunter Academy. "The home-educated kids of today are deprived," they lamented. "We were lucky to be on the ground floor of starting things like the senior high cruise, ski days, and graduation. With all the programs and classes that parents set up nowadays, do today's homeschooled teens have opportunities to implement their own ideas? Is there even room in their schedules to have time to dream up anything? It's no good if the grownups make it happen. The real fun is in doing for yourself."

Our educational philosophy was to teach the children to read, pray with them often, drive them to the library, and ask, "Really? Why? How come?" a lot. Mostly we stayed out of the way, letting the children themselves replace ignorance of a subject with knowledge and experience. It seems to have been successful. They have become fascinating adult friends.

GRANNY

Even though it is such an old-fashioned moniker, I prefer to be known as Granny both within and outside the family. Perhaps an excerpt from an e-mail by a son who was studying at the State University in Nizhni Novgorod, Russia (Gorky during the USSR era), will help to explain why.

"Saturday, January 23, 199_: Today is a lazy day. The only thing on the schedule is meals—which you MUST show up for. Something I learned very quickly here is about the babushka factor (babushka is the Russian word for grandmother). They will watch over you, care for you, literally dote on you, but never, EVER cross them! For instance, they will check you for hat, mittens and boots on a cold morning. They will assess you for signs of illness every day. If you are supposed to be present for a meal, be there. Babushkas remember the days when food was scarce and have no patience with waste or picky eaters. If you are late or skip, you will get the worst tongue-lashing you've ever heard. Of course you can't understand a word, but you definitely get the intent. *A babushka is always right*!"

Imagine that: a place in this world where age and experience still equate with authority and are thus automatically respected!

I came to greatly admire these elderly women while doing Bible smuggling/cultural exchange when Russia was still under Communist control. Clucking admonishments, cajoling laggards, the babushkas would bring queues of children to the parks when our drama team performed. They were always in motion, refocusing the youngsters' attention, bending to explain a concept, comforting a tired little child. They were opinionated, and sometimes irascible; I once saw a young military officer back off when a babushka glared at him! "Even if the parents don't know any better, I bring them and they (the children) will hear," one gray-haired woman fervently declared to me. She was determined that the children would hear the message of Christ's love.

I identify with the babushka spirit and share their mission. Nevertheless, in North America, the situation is different. How do elders show loving concern for the grandchildren without imposing advice on married children? At a luncheon some years ago, one guest asked us (then) younger women to talk about currently popular parenting styles since the practices of her generation were quite different from those her daughter-in-law employed. "It's much safer to question you than risk unintentionally insulting her," our friend explained.

So this Granny observes. Granny gets to slap her knee, laugh, and remind everyone that the present catastrophe is fodder for family reminiscence in a decade or so. Granny wants to empathize, yet has to zip lip unless asked and then attempts to deliver a proposition with tact and graciousness as from one friend to another. She prays that it will be received in that spirit, too. We Grannies have acquired a long view of life through the bumps and bruises of our parenting. Seeing disaster (or at least misadventure) in the making, we want to forestall the looming pain to our children and their kids. Nevertheless, perpetually, we must be like the mother of the bridegroom whose role is to offer no unsolicited suggestions, smile, and wear beige. Golly, it is hard! An American Granny is not always right.

BEGINNING

It would be nice to say that we began home-educating after much research and soul searching, but that would not be true. While I regretted the appearance of the yellow bus in our neighborhood, I never thought to challenge societal expectations that children, age five and older, disappeared from their families each day. We had decided upon a Christian elementary school for our daughter, thus, when our eldest son came of age, he too climbed aboard. I felt anew the pang that, just as my children became capable of partnering in really interesting activities, the law detached us. However, in time, circumstances changed the situation.

One morning the telephone rang. "We need to discuss your son's classroom placement and remedial reading program," began the headmaster of our children's school. "Inasmuch as he made good progress last year when you tutored him during that siege of mononucleosis, the board has considered his current situation and decided to designate your home as a satellite to the academy, with you, Pam, as primary instructor. Under these circumstances, we are confident the lad will quickly catch up with his classmates." Thus began our home-education adventure. Of course, the gentleman didn't anticipate our family falling in love with the home-education lifestyle nor subsequent children not entering classrooms until college.

We commenced with fairly high confidence knowing that the vision problems that had heretofore prevented our son from learning to read were largely corrected. Further, we had acquired a newly created, multisensory, phonics-based reading program from a skiing buddy of Jerry's who represented a major educational publisher. How innocent we were.

The reading textbook was supplemented with a teacher's manual containing a scripted presentation of the lessons. This style appealed to me as a neophyte educator. I would read the lesson dialogue, our son would answer, and shortly he would be reading on his own. Unfortunately, the manual omitted advice for what to do when the student didn't catch on to that scripted presentation. Mercifully, I discovered a 1950s-era volume designed for parents to assist their children with homework. Although not extensive in specific suggestions, it contained enough teaching principles and concept explanations to get us past the first round of frustrations. Ever since, I've collected teaching tips from anyone who instructs children.

Investing in pedagogy resources relieved my apprehensions plus showed me how to grow a student's competence rather than just jumping them through the next set of worksheet hoops. Asking the grandparents to give start-of-the-school-year gifts of specific titles was a way of swelling my library and building a multigenerational education team. Nowadays, there are many resources for parent-teachers with more coming every year.

Do procure one of the many books that provide an academic skill progression list. They can be an invaluable check that you are covering necessities. These are also helpful in ferreting out a weak link that is preventing competence with new material. Ruth Beechick's *You CAN Teach Your Child Successfully, Grades 4–8,* as well as her *The 3R's* series for grades K–3 are requisite classics.

Humble yourself to accept advice and mentoring from those with professional experience. Desperate, I delivered some of the children's writing assignments to a retired teacher friend for critique when student complaints that I was "way too hard!" became deafening. "Their protests are mostly justified," she agreed, then passed along age-appropriate expectations to employ when assessing the next set of papers.

There are other items I consider utterly necessary as well. Regular devotions, worship, and moment-by-moment prayer head the list. Next come library cards, generous storage shelves, and excellent lighting for all study and reading areas. A friend who will hear your worries without feeling compelled to fix them, plus let you cry or rejoice with empathy, will shield you from much burnout. Especially give yourself permission to demure when pressured to do anything that interferes with your full-time job of teacher.

Finally, for those with tiny children, a toddler kit of quiet, intriguing items only available during study time is essential. Rotate some objects weekly to preclude boredom. I learned a frightening lesson one morning when, having put the newborn down for a nap and shooed the "schoolie" out for fresh air, I took a bathroom break. I was greeted upon exit by the two-year-old's anxious, "Hot! Mama, BIG HOT!" interrupted by the smoke detector's alarm.

Longing for the tranquil routine now usurped by big and little brother's needs, our middle son had attempted to brew me a pot of tea "so you'll cozy me in da rocking chair with my picture books." Not wanting to be burned by the stove, he logically covered unoccupied surface units with hotpads. Not knowing which dial turned on the heat under the kettle, he twisted them all. The flames were quelled without fire department assistance, but, thereafter, my home-education lesson plans included entries for children of all ages.

WHERE ARE WE GOING?

With children, important questions come out of the blue. I remember only a couple of situations when I had a rehearsed speech ready. Usually someone beat me to the issue when I was least prepared. Commuting to a piano lesson one afternoon, a son, then in his early teens, zinged me with this volley:

"Our family believes that Jesus is God's son and we get salvation through him, right?"

"Correct."

"So we're Christians?"

"Each of us has made that decision, yes."

"You vote Republican, don't you?"

"I vote who seems to represent my views; often the candidate belongs to that party."

"Republicans are conservatives, aren't they?"

"Reputedly."

"Humph!" he settled against the car door and glared at me.

"You appear affronted and indignant," I observed, breathing deeply and wondering what had prompted this barrage. I was feeling especially curious as to what was coming next.

"Whatever," he muttered.

We rode in silence for a couple of minutes as I negotiated a freeway cloverleaf. Then he straightened up and turned towards me with earnest appeal on his face. "Well,

Mom, what I really want to know is this: if you really buy into what you just said, why are you and Dad so bent on us kids having a *liberal* arts education?"

Thus, cruising rush hour traffic on the interstate, I had to define "liberal" in education terms. Since my meaning—abundant and generous—ranks tenth among the definitions of liberal in *Webster's Unabridged Dictionary,* I understood our son's confusion. Looking an inch or so farther down the column, one can read the entry for "liberal arts" itself: academic instruction intended to provide general knowledge and comprising the arts, humanities, and natural sciences as opposed to professional or technical education. An ambitious reader who's gone to the end of that entry will also discover the word's etymology: [1745–55] translation of *L'artes liberales*—works befitting a free man. However, we hadn't considered any of these terms before embarking on our instructional activities. Our educational worldview honed over time.

Back when we were new home-educators, we parried inquiries of our motives by responding that we'd teach the children ourselves as long as it seemed to be working for them. Finessing the query, we'd smilingly quip, "We take it a year at a time." However, we reached a point when we knew that answer was a bluff and didn't satisfy us any better than it did our questioners. Quite acceptable norm-referenced test scores notwithstanding, were we truly cultivating our youngsters' mental soil as we'd envisioned?

Already regulars at the local coffee shop, our conversation now expanded. Besides discussing who needed additional practice in fractions or to speak more respectfully, we delved into our private educational philosophies. Specifically, how would we inculcate a belief system into our offspring? A thirst for knowledge? What had been redundant in our school careers? What had been left out? What sort of people did we hope our children would become? Above all, we wanted to avoid presenting an ad nauseum curricula of "read the book, answer the questions, take the test."

Eventually we wrote a set of reasons why various subjects were taught. Of practical benefit was that these statements provided a Dad-backed-up response when I was tweaked with that perennial student harassment, "What's the point in learning this?" All the response that was necessary was to point at the posted list.

The educational objectives of Hunter Academy:

Learn to manage yourself ... so you are free to become educated.

Learn to read ... it is the basis for everything else.

Learn to write and speak ... then you can impact the world.

Learn mathematics ... so you can manage your life.

Become knowledgeable in geography, science, literature and history ... so you can understand life and the world.

Develop your abilities in music, art, drama and sport ... so you can have healthy thrills in your life.

Become a person of prayer ... so you can always be taught by the Author of Life.

From these simple statements, we aspired to develop adventurous adults who were curious about all aspects of the world and not intimidated by obstacles—physical, spiritual, or human. We hoped they'd become confident people with judgement, albeit submitted to heavenly guidance, adequate to most any situation: persons who had wrestled with ideas enough that they might stand on their convictions without arrogance. We aspired to inspire individuals who would fill each minute with Kipling's "sixty seconds worth of distance run" and who couldn't be bored because they saw myriad horizons awaiting exploration or ways some service could be extended.

Putting flesh to our dream, we searched out materials that were decidedly unschoolish, preferring real-life practice sessions to those simulated in texts. Time to learn fundamental geometric formulas? After the procedure was introduced at the kitchen table, practice occurred on a vegetable garden that needed reconfiguring. Youth group mission trip in the offing? Research the destination's history, customs, literature, geography, and so on; then give the family an oral preview.

How did we know if they'd learned anything? Often by listening in on their conversations with visitors to our home. Were they "liberally" contributing to the discourse with age-appropriate comments laced with factoids and references to works read?

Our son came by the other day, offering to cook dinner. "I've discovered a new seasoning rub for fish," he confided. The table conversation traversed topics from a play he'd recently seen to scientific ethics to cabinet making. I was gratified at the breadth of his knowledge and the integrity of his opinions. "We want you to have a large mind," I'd told him in the car that long ago afternoon. "Therefore you need the broadest exposures we are able to provide for you and the deepest rigor you are capable of handling." Now long out of our nest, he personifies, indeed, a liberal education.

Lessons To Learn

The Daily Dozen
An Educational Goal
Hearth Quality
Winter
Thinking
Writing Assignments
Vocabulary Lesson
The Value of Memorizing
Testing Trials
Unit Study
Ohhhh, My!
Little Pitchers with Big Ears
What's in a Name?
Contentment
Another Educational Goal

THE DAILY DOZEN

It never seemed to fail. Just as I called the children to begin school, the cat coughed up a hairball (and its breakfast), the washer overflowed, the watertight integrity of the baby's diaper collapsed, or the phone rang. While turning off the ringer or turning on the answering machine easily remedied the last interruption, the others demanded more of my attention. We wanted initiative and responsibility to manifest in our pupils. To my consternation they sat idle, poked each other, and waited for direction, learning to hope for a mess so school could wait.

Something else needed addressing as well. It was apparent that the children were quickly grasping concepts. However, achieving instant recall of facts was another matter. While we would chide that "practice makes perfect," the kids really didn't connect how many repetitions are necessary for immediate response to occur.

Fortunately, all of them were taking music lessons and I gleaned some savvy strategies from their gifted teachers. As the children had grown more accomplished, they'd forgotten the amount of effort that had built the foundation of skills on which they now depended. Sometimes they balked at expending much energy to develop more dexterity. So their teachers played "Remember when you didn't know how to . . . ?" The teachers would help the children to recall that while tying shoes is now a no-brainer, how many times did the rabbit come up out of the hole and run around the tree and go back into his burrow before you got the hang of tying? Or, when reading, you now seldom need to sound out letter by letter or note by note. But did that *just happen*? Over and over and over they would remind the children that it takes lots of times through before you've really "got it."

The violin teacher assigned a weekly "Daily Dozen" of elements in pieces and short drills that built skills and, further, began to transfer practice session management from mother to student. Usually she would assign the number of repetitions based on age. "Let's see, you are seven now," whereupon young musician would interrupt to claim that actually he was nearly eight. "Well then, could you do this measure seven or, since you are getting so old, could you manage eight times each day? It really isn't much to do, is it?" she would beguilingly challenge.

I adopted her expression to start our mornings more productively. "Behold, the Hunter Academy Daily Dozen," I announced to the children. "Even if I'm delayed, you can get underway. Doing these straight off will get your brain in gear for the rest of the day."

All sorts of practices fit into the Daily Dozen category. And no, there weren't really twelve assignments, just a few. I wrote ungrammatical sentences on the blackboard; they proofread and corrected in their notebooks. Spelling words went on tape with earphones, ditto for history facts and vocabulary words, both foreign and English. With three-minute sand timers, they raced to complete a one-hundred-fact addition sheet; they received the same sheets each day until they had 100 percent accuracy. Then it was on to subtraction, multiplication, and division. Other choices were map labeling from memory, timed reading-comprehension pages from *The Reader's Digest,* and handwriting practice. Finally, the front page of the newspaper, recording weather data, and wildlife-birdfeeder observations rounded out the list. My selection criterion was simple: do-able projects that needed neither explanations nor my presence. Having a time pressure element helped to ignite sleepy minds.

If the Daily Dozen wasn't finished by the time the emergency was quelled, it was completed later while waiting for Mom to finish working with a sibling. Almost never could a child claim to have nothing to do. Some drills were graphed to chart progress and all were done with paper and pencil so proof of completion was evident (we employed broader modality methods at other times). The computer was off limits at this time of day until children had demonstrated consistent ability to work intently without supervision. Occasional, unannounced token rewards sustained enthusiasm and reinforced that growing maturity had pleasant consequences.

Organizing for the Daily Dozen took no special effort on my part as the materials were already on hand. The change was in when they were used. As weeks passed, study began routinely and fundamental skills and facts became automated. The best result was that the remainder of the day was freed up for genuine education to proceed.

An Educational Goal

I was present at a music recital to mind a young grand-daughter so her mommy could concentrate on her students. It was a nostalgic afternoon filled with images I'd seen many times before—a parent's nervousness exceeding that of her child; the ferocious concentration of some children; the mix of relief and pride as selections were completed. All were familiar. Unfortunately, during the reception afterwards, I overheard well-meant praises given to several young musicians, that anticipated life on the concert stage. A couple of our kids struggled with similar comments in their student days, but realistically, most children are not likely to turn pro. Besides, the fun of making music is reason enough to learn how.

Some of my fondest childhood memories are of the multigeneration sing-alongs that were a staple of our holiday celebrations. Since the instigator was my grandfather, who lived into his ninety-seventh year, the repertoire included lyrics from many decades. When we tired of singing, he would recite poetry. Born a Hoosier, he took delight in sharing the epics of James Whitcomb Riley, most of which he had committed to memory. The rest of us were expected to contribute to the entertainment as well, through instrument, song, and storytelling or even chanting the multiplication table.

Another set of recollections involves the impromptu orchestra that assembled after Sunday dinner at a family friend's home. Cacophony is a generous description of the "music" we produced. Children and adults, alike, traded around instruments, asking for quick playing tips and direction as to which staff to read. Hilarity attended mistakes and huzzahs reverberated when we sounded passable. The camaraderie of those afternoons instilled a sense of trust to risk less-than-perfect performance for the delight of attempting something new. Between gatherings, the desire to contribute more capably at the next get-together, spurred practice.

These experiences, unfortunately, seem odd to many folks. It seems as if, with the advent of recorded music a century ago, we have increasingly become a culture of music consumers rather than one of music makers. Furthermore, with editing, mixing, and dubbing so as to eliminate all glitches, it's easy to be intimidated. Just listening seems safer—and less work.

In parenting our brood, Jerry and I figured that if the kids had a lot of positive, soul-satisfying experiences, they wouldn't need to look for sinister excitement in less wholesome activities. Therefore, one of our educational goals was "develop skills in music, drama, art, and sport so you can have healthy thrills in your life." We told the kids that music skills are among the fundamental attributes of an educated person. Lessons were nonnegotiable. Believing as well that sound minds reside in sound bodies, developing life-sport capability meant another investment of energy. Consequently, there were years of winter Saturday mornings when we each set out with a pair of children dressed in ski togs; cocoa-filled thermos, lunch, and skis with

Jerry; instruments with me. Throughout the morning we'd shuttle them between the music conservatory in downtown Minneapolis and a close-in park where the Minneapolis Ski Club held a children's Nordic competition league.

Through all this activity, however, Colossians 3:23 was the goal: "Whatever you do, work at it with all your heart, as working for the Lord, not for men." When evaluating their progress, we wanted the children to consider more than mere skill acquisition—to focus, instead, on the Lord's standard of quality and to use their talents in ways that would draw others to Him. One son just missed being named to the National Junior Triathlon Team. He was able to swallow his disappointment more easily knowing that, among the six team members, there were young men like himself who saw it as a platform for sharing Jesus' love with people who were unlikely to come into a church.

Driving home from the recital, I hoped that the students at the concert would not let their level of recital performance rule the value of their music study. Applause is nice; dressing up is fun; recognition is gratifying; juice and cookies are a sweet reward. The lasting benefit of lessons comes in learning the intrinsic satisfactions of just trying, and in collaborating with others to simply enjoy the creative process.

HEARTH QUALITY

"Mmmm, that's hearth quality!" is code at our house for accomplishment. When a child learned something thoroughly, they stood on the stage of the fireplace hearth and performed for the family. Dessert afterwards completed the celebration. Occasionally, hearth quality occurred during practice time when, recognizing "I've really got this," they'd prance over to the brickwork to affirm their realization on the spot.

The mini-performances (which weren't limited to music) provided the stimulation of recitals without the pressure of an auditorium atmosphere. "Am I hearth quality, yet?" a seven-year-old asked hopefully looking up from reciting a poem in his McGuffy. It was the impetus for personal goal setting, as well. "In two weeks I'm gonna have this thing hearth quality," I overheard our twelve-year-old daughter declaring grimly to herself when one passage blocked mastery of a concerto. A couple of decades later, when she and her husband bought a home, her excited description detailed a landing two treads up the curving staircase of the hundred-year-old house. "Even if you don't have a fireplace, there's still a spot for hearth-quality performances," we enthused with her.

Hearth quality, however, only meant something was as well polished as it was apt to be at this stage of a child's development. As adults, we knew celebrations of progress were absolutely needed since perfection, if it ever came, would be a while arriving. Naively expecting to be pros after six lessons, the children were often frustrated and discouraged at how long it was going to take to get good.

Learning to enjoy the journey also spilled into academic lessons. "Stop a second," I'd suggest at "Ah-ha!" moments, "How do you feel? Savor your success!" Once, on vacation, we watched the delirious bliss of a dog rolling in the seaweed and other smelly accumulation along the high-tide line of an ocean beach. "That's the kind of pleasure you want to suck in when your work is well learned," we winked at the kids.

We hoped to inculcate the private glee that emanates from knowing that you have conquered a bit of knowledge. So encouragements such as "You're getting there," "Yessssss!" "You tried," "It is better," were offered at the slightest hint of improvement or in acknowledgement of repetitions dutifully completed. Sometimes we'd get a jaunty "Yep!" in return; sometimes a sullen "Yeah,"—a huge cue to provide a hug or sympathetic nod delivered silently lest more parental words tempt them to defend (and entrench) their negative assessment.

Hearth quality wasn't praise time because praise implies a pedestal from which you can topple. It was time to bask in the accomplishment of the present. Therefore we championed effort even when progress was at a plateau. Making uninterrupted headway isn't typical. People stall. Hearth quality let the children treasure a tiny skill that would have gone unnoticed in a recital or at a project night. Nevertheless, hearth quality wasn't a sop—you did have to know your stuff. But for the timid or discouraged, having a forum to display even a small harvest gleaned from perseverance was profitable.

Last Thanksgiving our family's next generation mounted the hearth to let everyone see the results of the initial three weeks of musical labor. At Christmas, the stairwell landing showcased more development. But even without hearths or landings, hopefully every home can have a celebration spot for delighting in skills acquired and goals on the way to being attained.

WINTER

The looooong stretch begins when we change calendars. The season of blahs, cabin fever, and temper has come. Our first two Minnesota winters were consumed settling into a new home, then producing a second child. We were too busy to notice if the weather affected us. However, the next February brought near-record low temperatures and I learned about cabin fever. While Jerry worked in Phoenix for extended periods, our even-tempered three-and-a-half-year-old turned into a shrew, and the eight-month-old pillaged as neo-Attila the Hun. Then came clemency.

"Get on the first flight you can find," Jerry ordered. "This trip they've put us up in a garden apartment complex. A crib is ordered and the pool is just outside." With sunshine, a play yard, room for running, and hours in that pool, cheerful attitudes resumed. Returning to Minnesota, we purchased a heavily discounted, preschool jungle gym, filled the wading pool with sand, and lashed plywood to an old bedspring as a trampoline. The basement became a vigorous activity center—for we'd come to realize that the children's undesirable behavior had a physical base and wasn't entirely a deficit of character training.

When we began our home-based education adventures, that February lesson was incorporated into the lesson plan. Between Christmas and Easter there are only minor celebrations. It's the longest uninterrupted teaching time of the year. Textbook writers take advantage of this by presenting most of the new material during this period. Fall is the time to solidify last year's lessons; spring previews next winter's topics. It is a sequence that has worked successfully for generations. In the upper Midwest, with daylight-short days, winter session can seem interminable to a kid. Konos author, Jessica Hulcy, admonishes that God put the wiggle in children and our job as parent-educators is to work with it, not take it out of them. Seatwork alternated with large-muscle activity lets bodies un-kink. We permitted our ski-jumper sons three rides on their backyard practice snow bump each time an assignment was completed before the timer's chime.

The stale atmosphere of well-insulated houses can have a depressive effect, so hourly our kids were sent to gulp fresh air on the porch. Daily, we got outside to absorb sunshine to renew vitamin D levels and prevent seasonal affective disorder (the children thought we went to sled, ski, or skate). Long winter climates necessitate special planning if optimal education is to happen.

Embrace the season, and use it to educational advantage. Besides the obvious activities mentioned above, consider playing croquet or golf in the snow (use colored balls) or learn to snowshoe, a skill that even toddlers can accomplish and is much less expensive than skiing. Extend science lessons by tracking paw prints of backyard wildlife and recording bird feeder visiting patterns. Math becomes meaningful with activities such as measuring snowfall amounts then comparing those to day-old, settled depths, or melting a uniform volume of the white stuff after each storm to determine its moisture content. Consider conducting a contest to predict spring runoff volume and river flooding possibilities based on these calculations.

Guessing the "ice-out" date for lakes is a venerable upper Midwest tradition, but your students, using almanacs and researching the newspaper archives at the library, can make educated prognostications. Collect, play, and sing music relating to winter; recite poetry with a winter theme. You can have the children practice during commutes to field trips. Build snow sculptures relating to indoor lessons or make a yard-sized map of the current country in geography and "travel" through it, narrating events, land features, and important products. Even when the temperature drops off the thermometer, keep those bodies moving. Then winter doldrums and cooped-up crankies will largely bypass your family's school.

THINKING

If there is one word we use day in and day out while working with our students, it is "think." So much of our time and effort is spent trying to get our children to think about, think through, think before acting, think before speaking.

To give the opportunity for development of our children's thinking, we declared that eating dinner together was a unwavering ritual in our home. Music lessons, sport practices, and other activities had to fit around the nightly gathering. We laid out full place settings, though plastic glasses and junior-sized flatware accommodated immature coordination, lit a candle, and required shirts, combed hair, and scrubbed faces. Initially, the children did not enjoy this modest attempt at formality but when they got into their teen years and could confidently face etiquette and protocol situations, they were grateful. More important, however, than the food or trappings, was the conversation that flowed across that table.

Of course everyone was expected to share the highlights and low-lights of their day. Furthermore, as soon as a child could decode, he was responsible for at least the headlines in the publications to which we subscribed. Between *God's World*, various secular liberal and conservative magazines, *Minnesota Christian Chronicle, Pro Family News,* and the local paper, many points of view were available for debate and dissection. Even seven-and eight-year-olds learned they could offer opinions and spout, "I read where ... "

On nights when mouths chewed more than they spoke, we'd play "Word," a vocabulary-building game of taking turns randomly cracking the dictionary, pronouncing an entry, then giving the real definition or a wildly inaccurate yet plausible-sounding made-up one. The family would consider, and perhaps challenge, the veracity of the explanation with applause awarded for their fashioning a clever definition or for being in the right when suspicions were aroused. In either case, our children learned to keep a straight face and be nimble in their use of language.

The best meals, though, involved discussing tough topics: those moral issues and life dilemmas where right isn't always clear; when no matter which tack you chose, hurt may result for someone. Sometimes we'd start with "tell us what 'other kids are thinking,'" which permitted our children to share anonymously any personal struggles too. Other times we asked questions that we suspected nobody else would ask them. "Why the anger? What keeps us doing what we say shouldn't be done?" Nothing was off limits. Broad, open-ended questions aren't so threatening and they encourage children to open up and talk. Once questions were posed, we learned to stop talking ourselves and just listen.

The point of our discourse wasn't to solve anything on the spot, but it did help get the pulse of our children's world both within and beyond the family. For example, there was the spring evening the boys gave the girls an earful about what slit-skirts, shorts, and low necklines did to their resolve to maintain a pure thought life.

Plaintive questions emerged: What *is* my responsibility for running errands or driving friends home; am I really serving or just enabling folks to practice irresponsibility in their planning? Or, the Scout troop's next project is distributing organ donation cards and I'm not sure I believe in transplants. Do I have to participate? Or, non-Christians have invited me to their party; there may be beer. What is the stronger witness, stay away, and stay pure; or go, not drink, and develop relationships?

Conversations on big questions don't resolve quickly or tidily, a reality we also wanted to convey. Pat answers, platitudes, and legalisms stop thinking. We'd keep the dialogue moving with phrases such as "Hmmm, hadn't thought of it that way." "I've wondered about that, too." "Keeeeep talking." "What else do they say?" "This a concern, isn't it?" There's no easy answer, is there?"

The lesson intended was that intelligent people can discuss anything with dignity and composure. It's OK to argue and amazing to discover minutes later that you and a sibling are on the same page with a different subject. Disagreeing doesn't equate to demonizing. Our dinner conversation was designed to be a boxing ring for ideas so skills could sprout in a trusting atmosphere. Jerry and I tried very hard to never use dinner talk as an opportunity to lecture (a sure turnoff to future discussions) and everyone's opinion was respected. As Samuel Johnson put it, "That is the happiest conversation where there is no competition, no vanity, but a calm quiet interchange of sentiments."

WRITING ASSIGNMENTS

"Mooommmm! Do I have to? I can't think of any-thing. It sounds dumb. I HATE writing." Heard such kid-noise at your house? What drove me 'round the bend was children staring at the pristine sheet until the timer chimed the next subject. I called the syndrome "blank-paper-itis" and it sucked teaching enthusiasm right out of this parent. Truthfully, writing is hard work. Trouble is, few people ever get enough practice jotting thoughts to discover they have competency for routine writing needs, let alone real-ize that they have a knack for communicating on paper.

In this twenty-first century of PCs and e-mail, rapidly produced, effectively written communication is essential in every vocation. From birth, spoken language is modeled to children, yet rarely do they see adults with pen in hand. The grocery or a chore list seems like the limit of parental writing, although, infrequently, they might observe a consumer complaint letter being written. Short term, the telephone seems more efficient. In terms of teaching com-position, that expediency is costly. We all have to over-come writing aversion.

Teaching the kids to write didn't come easily. We tried many suggestions and programs, among them journaling, choosing topics from published lists, and analytical pre-sentations of writing techniques. None of these were effective for us. Finally, we realized the children needed both a personal reason to fuel their writing project and a prototype to imitate. So, we introduced "Why I ..." as a pattern for papers. Every essay follows this formula: thesis/introduction, at least three "whys" (supporting statements, each distinctly different from each other), and conclusion. Whether the format is the high school five-paragraph-essay, college research paper, or even a book or sermon, it's the same sequence although the length differs.

Here's an example:

I would like to have a dog. (Thesis)

I could learn responsibility by caring for a dog. (Point 1)

Dogs provide companionship. (Point 2)

If a dog lived here, our house would be safe from crime. (Point 3)

For these reasons, I believe that I should be allowed to get a dog. (Conclusion)

Scanty as this paragraph appears, it makes a logical, clear argument. The fundamental "Why I ..." is achievable by eight-year-olds. "Why I ..." strategy by passes the mind-numbing glare of that empty sheet of paper. Over time, we created subject-specific templates for reports and even thank-you letters. Filling in template blanks kickstarts children's thinking and reduces worry over failure. Of course, the paragraph should be enhanced with details. This happened naturally as the children grew older and more skillful. Usually, I'd suggest each point be put on a separate page so there was plenty of space for experimenting and improving. A highlighter pen illuminated final word choices for recopy time.

Occasionally I'd take dictation from a struggling writer as a boost to their getting their thoughts onto paper. Organizing ideas in our heads, then transmitting thoughts from brain through fingers along a pencil (wielded with sufficient dexterity to ensure legibility) is a complex procedure. One of our languishing students wrote more easily after we acquired a word processor.

Beside dogs, everything became fodder for papers: a new ball mitt, a snowboard, bedtime, their own room, a chore-chart responsibility. To vexing questions (invariably posed when I was wrist-deep in a mess) I had a ready response, "There's your next assignment." Writing now had purpose.

Good writing is not an extemporaneous activity. Thoughtlessly, I hadn't been providing an extended time for projects. In fifteen or even thirty minutes, you don't get warmed up much less surmount the inevitable false starts and discarded phrases that are normal events in producing a paper. Therefore, in the elementary years (which was when the bulk of how-to instruction occurred), I cleared Wednesday morning for Writer's Workshop. This let the children get into their "zone", to borrow an athletic term, besides providing opportunity to solicit suggestions and share excerpts with each other. Furthermore, Mom wrote, too—notetaking from homeschooling books, letters, occasionally articles for publication. A clutch of freshly sharpened pencils and unlimited mugs of cocoa lent a celebratory atmosphere to the morning. They wrote the rest of the week, too, sometimes sketching out ideas via mind maps and quickie outlines, other days pressing to complete a composition.

Finally, what children read or hear read to them influences the caliber of what they write. It is natural to emulate the authors to whom you are exposed. While a few children may be intimidated by mature literary language, others relish mimicking, producing bloated, pretentious sentences. But hyperbole is an improvement over sourfaced scratchings. As with any skill, practice is the key. "Guys, it's like math facts or shooting hoops," I'd repeat, "you have to do it and do it until it becomes instinctive." And, eventually it did.

Vocabulary Lesson

Two red-haired foxes will scamper through the house this Christmas, a sight we have been anticipating since an e-mail came from Russia last winter. "Shhh, don't let on to the nieces, but I found perfect gifts for them at the Izmilovski Park Bazaar yesterday. They'll have warm heads the next time the snow flies!" So after the preening and parading that little girls seem born knowing how to perform, we adults are braced for growls and requests for much petting by the now furry-hatted ones.

Children recognize early the persona a head covering confers; a *hat* turns you into somebody or something. The king wears a *crown*, we inform baby as we look through a board book together. An astronaut has a bubble *helmet*; the nurse pins on a white *cap*; the cowboy wears a *Stetson*. A few years later a hat identifies aspirations, "I'm a fireman!" or shows membership, "I'm in Scouts, see my cap?"

Time was when the type of hat worn denoted a student's year in school—although Jerry's and my college did abolish the *freshman beanie* the fall I matriculated. *Mortarboards* continue to mark successful completion of graduation requirements. Mercifully, *dunce caps* are no more. Nonetheless, some hats could assist your student's studies (at least they could be helpful if presented light-heartedly, never in shame or as punishment). A pair of *earmuffs* might benefit an auditory distractible student. Even if sounds are not entirely quelled, the muffs remind the student of the need to ignore the classroom buzz. An old fashioned *bonnet* focuses eyes on pesky math problems rather than roving to a sibling's antics. A *sweatband* signifies the need for perseverance when editing the third (or sixth draft?) of an assignment.

How many kinds of hats can you name? *Fedora, fez, balaclava,* and *tam o'shanter* are regularly seen by children but do they label them as such? Learning precise terms for familiar items as a young child sets the expectation that there are equally exact names in other bodies of knowledge. Besides, it is empowering to know "big" names for things. Literature abounds with descriptive head coverings that are often critical to understanding the nuances of the story. *Stocking, nightcap, bonnet, sombrero,* and *coonskin* are probably familiar. Do your children know *chapeau, derby, snood, wimple, stovepipe, pillbox, beret, kerchief, Homburg, bandanna, petasus, turban, coif, yarmulke, tricorne, caul, Panama,* or *Bowler*? Are there additional hat names not mentioned here? These italicized words might provide the impetus for a dictionary/encyclopedia assignment followed by a sketching session to render facsimiles of the research. Which hat would you like to wear? From which country and historical period does each hat come? How do you think it got the name it has?

I had to consciously make a mental transfer of my "hat" twice a day when we were home-educating. If I didn't, I often deprived my children of the clean slate they deserved when beginning their daily studies. The atmosphere was fouled when my nagging about homework carried over into homeschool and vice versa. Also, a classroom worn "mom-hat" allowed more leniency on due dates or recitation quality than was justified. For us, it worked better if mom stayed home and teacher, pulling on her *academic hood*, came to school.

THE VALUE OF MEMORIZING

A faculty mantra of my elementary school was that being able to recite poems would be advantageous throughout our lives. Consequently, not mere couplets, but midsize epics were assigned, as well as patriotic speeches and multiple-verse songs. Singing in an oratorio society for many years also committed considerable scripture to my musical memory. Those teachers' instincts were correct, although I doubt they envisioned the exceptional impact on my life.

In the mid-eighties, our family was part of an international peace program that brought citizen-level, cross-country skiers from the Soviet Union to Minnesota for participation in local races. One evening, after partaking of impromptu Thanksgiving dinners in the various host homes, we gathered to share other aspects of our cultures. The Russians were amazing! One after the other they rose to narrate a story, or recite Pushkin and other poets. Most delightful was their singing: lusty, loud, and lengthy tunes. It was embarrassing for us Americans. Collectively we came up with just a couple of ditties, *"If I Had A Hammer"* and *"I've Been Working on the Railroad,"* to which everyone could remember the words. Only our family's children were prepared to recite anything. By the next year, Jerry and I had printed a collection of truly representative American offerings, gleaned out of remembered assignments, from which we and the other host families performed, then gave to our guests as souvenirs.

Those early years of memorizing held another benefit for me. As a young adult, praying for release from the night terrors that had plagued my sleep since childhood, I asked the Lord to refill my slumber with His truth. Ever since, it is a rare morning that I awaken without scripture in my mind... often set to music. Therefore, at dawn, September 11, 2001, the alarm and a passage from Mendelssohn's *Elijah* were a counterpoint as I opened my eyes: "He, watching over Israel, slumbers not, nor sleeps. Shouldst thou, walking in grief, languish; He will quicken thee." I wondered briefly as to the application of those particular words, prayed that they would manifest where needed and got dressed.

Check-in at the Minneapolis airport an hour later was routine. Waiting for my monthly flight to the West Coast to look in on my parents, I sat in the business center where I can get some writing done in a quiet atmosphere. Emerging to find my gate, I caught the last words of the chilling announcement declaring a national emergency, looked out the terminal's windows and saw the sky filled with ships on rapid descent. But as the horrifying news made its way through my senses from simple hearing to comprehension, the dawn melody returned to my consciousness. Utter calm enveloped me even as the second announcement—to collect checked luggage and evacuate the terminal immediately—came across the PA system.

Nonetheless, riding back to our house with the radio broadcasting grisly details, that initial peace began to shatter. A verse from a childhood poetry assignment put emotion into words: "Then in despair, I bowed my head, 'There is no peace on earth,' I said. 'For hate is strong and mocks the song of peace on earth, good will to men.'" Those words were reinforced throughout the day as we sat glued to the grim television coverage.

In late evening, needing fresh air and a stretch before retiring, I walked onto the deck, but phantom images of our toddler grandson and his daddy innocently playing in the backyard while on stateside leave a few weeks earlier assailed my thoughts. Apprehension for this eldest son, whose Army career has already sent him into some of the nastiest situations of the past twelve years, spilled into tears. And yet, my "What if?" questions were stilled by the final verse of Henry Wadsworth Longfellow's poem, echoing the theme of the now long ago morning song: "Then pealed the bells more loud and deep: 'God is not dead, nor does He sleep. The wrong shall fail, the right prevail, with peace on earth, good will to men.'"

You may recognize this poem as stanzas of a Christmas hymn set to the music of J. Baptiste Calkin. Make a priority to build in your children such a reservoir of scripture, music, and literature so as to flow unbidden with words to rouse, sustain, or comfort when the times of life overwhelm. How I bless those wise teachers of my childhood for the legacy they gave me!

TESTING TRIALS

One week in late winter I sat beside our seven-year-old in a Christian school classroom while a norm-referenced test was proctored. It became obvious that disaster was in the making. This student was already at a disadvantage since decoding simple words was a quite recently acquired skill. My heart climbed even higher into my throat as I observed that my child was just randomly blacking in the ovals on the answer sheet and when I was momentarily distracted, turned over three pages and began bubbling spaces in an entirely different test section.

Although the headmaster of this institution had suggested homeschooling to us to meet the needs of one of our older children, when we expanded to include more von Gohrens, eyebrows were raised. I was convinced that the reputation of home education was at stake based on our children's success level on these examinations. In those days there were no reassuring statistics about home-schooling. We had a gut conviction that this style of education would work. At the moment my gut was twisted in panic. Prosecution of home educators was rampant; in fact, testing the children was to provide documentation that they were being adequately educated.

As proof that the Lord does protect his "chicks," the scores I picked up a few weeks later were gratifying, although it took many minutes before my hands stopped shaking enough to read them. Even the random bubbler had achieved slightly above the fiftieth percentile on the complete battery.

On the other hand, a troublesome issue manifested in the older children. With some scores in the PHS (post-high school) range, their motivation dropped. "Why should I continue to study when I am post-high school?" Warm weather had arrived; they were convinced that, as testing was over, vacation should begin. After we educated them on norm-referenced test terminology, they were chagrined that they weren't off the hook. Even so, we all felt smug. They had done as well in those PHS sections as someone who had graduated from high school would have been expected to score if they had taken the very same grade level of the test.

At the same time, I determined that I never wanted to go through such an emotionally wrenching experience again, so I educated myself about testing options. After finding another source for norm-referenced tests, I also discovered that these tests are normed to three separate periods in the calendar year. Testing in the fall, winter, or spring carries no penalty or advantage over another time. I quickly decided that having fresh results in the fall, rather than old scores carried from the previous spring, was educationally beneficial for this teacher. The date change would also squash the children's expectation that once the tests were completed, school was out.

We settled on the last week of September as our test window. Employing the challenge, "You do want to do well on your tests, of course," as a motivator, review and drill became the first task of each school year. Not only did this establish a routine in our academy, but lesson preparation was lighter so my fall canning and freezing chores weren't compromised. Besides, there was a plentiful supply of testing instruments available at the early date.

In short, taking the norm-referenced tests in autumn kick-started our year. Once they were over, we could get on with the real business of education.

To quell my perfectionist fears of whether I'd passed or failed as a teacher based on those test scores, I listened closely to the description by an older child of the test day atmosphere in another classroom of that Christian school. Besides opening with prayer each morning, the teacher dressed in cheerleading sweaters from her own school days and led the class in enthusiastic rousers that convinced them to try their hardest on every sub-test. At the conclusion of the final day, the children were urged to jump, whoop, holler, and praise God that they were done. Quite a few test booklets got tossed heavenward, too, I was told. Never having been on a pep squad, I lacked the clothing, but cheering and clanging our Tyrolian cowbell was possible.

After *our* toss and stomp dance, we departed for the ice cream shop to celebrate having completed the annual "rendering unto Caesar." Norm-referenced testing had been placed in appropriate perspective: it is hardly a full educational portrait, just a quick snapshot to mark progress in some areas.

Unit Study

It wasn't the jumbled disarray of furniture or the walls denuded of fifteen years of posters that got to me. While the abandoned bear puppet made me gulp—there was a time when our son had wondered if he could ever be without his Blackie—it wasn't until I sank into the easy chair in his former reading corner and glanced at the underside of the sleeping loft that the finality of this adult child leaving home hit me. Above me, carefully secured, but available for reference, was the scaled floor plan drawing of what became his teenage room.

The unit study had been called "A Man's Home is His Castle." It was really an ancient civilization history overview but that title would never intrigue a couple of middle school sons. "Suppose we approach this from an architectural perspective?" I queried Jerry. "Making models of construction breakthroughs like arches, domes, flying buttresses, and trusses might spark enthusiasm for discovering why people lived and behaved as they did. If we integrate decorative art study and skills like painting, room function, and furniture arrangement, they could practice by updating their bedrooms."

Tacked above my head was culmination of the latter aspect of that education experience. "What needs does my castle have to meet?" headlined the graph paper room layout. Charted alongside were columns, Function, Wishes,

Decision; and entries, Sleep: more floor space—loft the bed; Entertainment: train board—loft the bed; Bookshelves: convenient—in loft; Mess making: storage, LOTS!—new closet setup; Bright colors/posters: LOTS!—white walls. It was a feat to build that loft into a standard bedroom. However, much learning in mathematics, physics, engineering, and visual art was accomplished during the project and, in solving their bedroom problems, the boys indeed identified with issues, practices, and solutions of people long ago.

By mid-January, our refrigerator held sheets of paper on which the children listed things they wanted to learn about in the coming year. It was a long time until September but I needed this information ahead of home-ed conferences and used book sales. Studying topics that fascinated them bore greater skill-fruit than traditional subjects and developed scholarship, not academic hoop jumping.

The lists were up only a couple of weeks, after which I spent some evenings praying and perusing them for any kind of common threads; also, for logical connections to knowledge that we parents knew they needed to acquire. Then I would show the librarian the directions the kids wanted to pursue, and the fun of finding materials began. Yes, it took effort, but for myself, that was preferable to popping headache remedies after answering "Why do I have to learn . . . ?" grouches. During final planning in August, I referred to sequential competency lists to be sure that appropriate skill acquisitions were incorporated. We used textbooks to provide a skeleton for some units, but paramount was to teach the child, not merely teach a course or a book.

Of course, there are now integrated theme units commercially available. However, creating our own allowed true customization and some unique twists. Besides historical, scientific, and other facts, we encouraged squirreling away useful daily living nuggets as well. In an economics unit, the kids were challenged to purchase the most vacuum cleaner they could get for the dollars we'd budgeted. First came consumer research, then field investigations. The salespeople's smiles faded as our team ground their own test materials (a baggie of dog hair, another of thread snippets, and one of tiny paper scraps) into the demo carpets. A national sales director, introducing a new hire to his territory, spotted our activity. Intrigued, he asked if he could answer questions, then gave the children forty-five minutes of shopping tips and demonstrations. When we came back to make our purchase, we learned that he had set aside a discontinued top-end model with instructions to sell it to our children at whatever their budget permitted.

That vacuum now stood across the room ready to suck up spackle dust. The old bedroom was destined for a new role; cleaning and painting were ahead. It had been a good place for a boy to become a man.

Oʜʜʜ, Mʏ!

Some clever families keep a loaded camera handy that is dedicated to daily chronicling their education activities. This ingenious documentation attests to the scope and constancy of their curriculum. Though not as diligent as the aforementioned parents, we, too, exposed numerous rolls through the years. Many of the best snapshots, however, are those Jerry and I have squirreled away in the personal album of our minds.

No film records the morning I found an eighteen-month-old seated in the cave of the fireplace showering herself with week-old ashes and murmuring "snow!" Nor was a camera nearby when a slightly younger child made an early dinner of the cat's supper while moussing hair and fur with fish-flavored goo—just before we were to eat out at a restaurant.

There is a photo, however, of a mud-covered son, who, unable to wait any longer for the beach season to begin, went swimming in the frog pond the day after the ice went off.

Thankfully, no depiction exists of a dinner table teasing that resulted (I still swear it was accidental) in Mom pegging Dad squarely on his forehead with a spoon, drawing blood, and flabbergasting the children. "I'm leaking," was Jerry's wondering comment as he gazed at the now bloodstained hand he'd raised to ward off my missile.

Ours is an "Ohhh, my ..." family, we have concluded, rather than an "OH-MY-GOSH!" clan, although initially this was not so. As young parents we were easily alarmed, reacting to many things as catastrophes. Frankly, hyper-adrenaline living proved exhausting. Besides, a week later we usually were laughing over the mistakes, blunders, antics, oversights, and slip-ups. Eventually we saw the humorous more quickly. When we couldn't laugh, we would sigh, trusting that if we hung in "it" would be over soon.

The OH-MY-GOSH! style had led to "awful-izing" thought patterns: What if? What's next? I can't cope!!! Then we were deafened and blinded to reasonable solutions as well as to the teachable moments a situation presented. "What will best prepare our children to unriddle adulthood?" we asked ourselves, "Knee-jerk emotion or a measured response?" We didn't shrug off the implications of decoding concepts *still* not comprehended, a threatening letter from the school district, blood, or fire. However, when ground zeros occurred, instead of instantly blowing, it really did help to first draw a deep breath (or two or six) and give the Lord some moments to speak calm into the situation.

Children adopt whatever behavior they observe when problems crop up. Will it be shrieks, wails, or brainwork? Learning to recite aloud my mental processing as I considered alternatives and devised remedies lessened thoughtless reactions while providing my pupils with tools for future use.

One Christmas the nineteen-month-old maneuvered to "see da baby Jesus" in the crèche placed on top of a mid-height bookcase. Of course he fell, splitting his fore-head on the shelves. Eight-year-old brother was first on the rescue scene. "Grandma, get ice! Grandpa, get a towel," he commanded (I was at music lessons with the siblings and Jerry was on an airplane). To our son's consternation, the visiting grandparents came running, instead. "I need you to help, not worry," he admonished them, to my father's admiring amusement.

Now that lad has become a father himself. Three weeks before baby's arrival, we held a trans-Atlantic telephone conversation. "The enormousness of what we've gotten ourselves into is beginning to hit home," he admitted. "Still, I'm thinking most about all the things we are going to do together and the stories we'll tell and the adventures we'll have." As my camera recorded baby's homecoming and their first days as new parents, I saw signs that his will be an "Ohhh, my ..." family, too.

LITTLE PITCHERS WITH BIG EARS

Sprawled beside the glowing coals of the beachside bonfire, my parents' and their companions' conversation segued into gossip about their children. I lay nearby in the shadows feigning sleep. In my twelve years, I'd learned an important principle: adults speak candidly when children aren't obviously present. That's when eavesdropping youngsters learn what their parents really believe about their offspring. At least they imagine they do.

The Scotsman, Robert Burns, wrote, "O wad some Pow'r the giftie gie us, To see oursels as others see us!" Listening to adult conversations has profound impact on children. It tends to confirm their suspicions about what is valued in them. Alternatively, comments may challenge an inbred negative belief system. Eventually I acquired a label for my childhood axiom. The professor called it "referential speaking." It's utterly simple and strongly affects behavior.

Referential speaking involves those comments that children hear about themselves and take to heart for good or ill. These statements are neither praise nor affirmations. They aren't directed at the child, either. Rather, they make positive reference about the child to other adults. The words are spoken in the spirit of Proverbs 16:23-24: "A wise man's heart guides his mouth, and his lips promote instruction. Pleasant words are a honeycomb, sweet to the soul and healing to the bones."

When parents choose their words to set realistic expectations or make positive observations, growth results. For instance, a shy child, hearing a comment about her kindness in speaking to a newcomer at the field trip, may take courage that she can approach a stranger another time. The mother-deaf child who must be nagged will prick up his ears when mom talks about how helpful he was while dad was traveling. The whiner needs to overhear genuine recognition of signs of budding maturation. As long as kids don't sense manipulation, they'll put credence in frank remarks.

Conversely, dismayed sighs are not likely to stimulate improvement in a son who is "always" late with assignments or a daughter who "never" seems to get math concepts. The opposite may actually take place. Aggravated utterances are apt to convince children that they certainly are hopeless. They may even give children a perverse sense of power—their problem can't be cured. Then achievement short of true ability cements into disappointing habit.

Another aspect to parental speaking needs illumination. The kinds of references that adults make about their employment or volunteer work also affects children's achievement. If we martyr over unappreciated efforts at church or in the community, do we mean to imply that acts of mercy or help to neighbors aren't worth our exertions? When we drag home, griping about the intelligence of a supervisor or the impossible timeline of a project, do we truly intend to communicate that adult work and responsibility are onerous? To be avoided? Although the aphorism reads that what we do speaks louder than what we say, in this case, the reverse is more accurate.

Of course dad or mom may be seeking helpful suggestions to resolve a perplexing situation. Perhaps they are actually asking for confirmation that their burden, though heavy, has value. But without interpretation, children may assess parental candor as bitter hopelessness and adopt a similar posture. When the grownup's homecoming litany frequently expresses craving for weekends with nothing to do but play or vegetate, then what is conveyed to children is that adulthood is overwhelming and maturity is not worth aspiring to. Those are unfortunate messages for children to internalize. Thoughtless referential speaking can set the stage for school attitudes that demand all learning to be effortless entertainment.

Implementation of referential speaking isn't difficult, although it means attending to one's word choices. (At first, I rehearsed phrases in the shower.) The trick is to tell someone intentionally, though casually, about what you want reinforced. Genuinely exclaim or contentedly gloat in your dialogue. If there is no one around with whom to converse, you can use this gambit. Once in a great while I would telephone myself and have a one-sided conversation to provide opportunity for a child to listen in. Recently, I owned up to this subterfuge with an adult son. While stunned that he'd been taken in, he laughingly divulged he'd deliberately hovered near the phone in hopes of picking up any secrets that mom might blurt out about him. "You know it did work, Mom. We believed what you said about us to other folks a whole lot more than what you said directly to us!" he confessed.

At the same time, ignore or greatly limit verbalizing about what's negative. Of course, you and your spouse need to talk over and plan how you will remedy childishness and inexperience, but do this out of the kids' earshot. Jerry and I used to go for coffee at an all-night restaurant or take a private walk for discussions. When we disciplined ourselves to be conscious of our referential speaking, we saw a difference in the atmosphere of our home and our academy. Little pitchers have big ears. It was worth the effort to fill them with inspiring, positive expectations.

What's in a Name?

"Granny, why me have *one* name?" the two-and-a-half-year-old voice quavered and eyes were brimful. "Mommy has two names and you has three," (huge woe-begone sigh) "but me just has one." What? Two names? Three? Then I got it. "Oh, Darling, you have lots of names!" I exclaimed, and began explaining about titles (mommy/granny) then middle and family names. We remembered nicknames as well; sometimes she is Little Puss, Punkin, Snooks, a Big Helper, and so on. Tears evaporated upon the assurance that Granny would use her first AND middle name whenever she desired.

At an exposition of Native American quilts, I saw photos of a Hopi naming ceremony with three-month-olds cushioned on waist-high stacks of fluffy piecework. A prayerfully selected attribute name, it seems, accompanies each quilted gift to bless the child's future spiritually and materially. When our grandson was born, his parents, acknowledging his mother's Korean heritage, held a party one hundred days after his birth. It is then that the infant is named and welcomed by friends and extended family.

An African proverb proclaims that a child who has many names is a child who is much loved. We put much thought into the formal name on each child's birth certificate; however, what we dubbed them day-to-day distinguished their place in our hearts. In time each child had an animal name (Puss, Lion, Bear, Tiger), various German and American diminutives *(liebschen, schatzie,* sweetie, honey, big fella), and, as they got older, we consciously adopted functional names (trooper, sport, right-hand, sleuth, dependable, problem-solver, wise one, friend). One evening we started recounting everybody's appellations and were delightedly amazed at the extensive lists.

Few folks deliberately give negative labels to their children and if they do so accidentally, smart parents apologize quickly. But when we are on the telephone, conversing at field trips or gathered around the fellowship hall coffee urn, kids overhear their parents refer to them and what they hear can be problematic. That they are a slow learner or a late bloomer or poky, stingy, egotistical, or just like some relative, may be true. However, children, having a fuzzy understanding of such terms, catch the emotion-filled parental voice and latch onto the identity. Our unguarded epithets are often embraced more fully than the names we carefully chose for their christening. These become titles that, in their immaturity, children tend to live up to, not rise above.

What do you hope for your child? Are your references about them a blessing or, inadvertently, a curse? If our offspring are to fulfill the heavenly call on their lives, we must soberly assess their qualities and also correct our judgments. Once a professor had us write single-word descriptions of children's negative characteristics. Then we were instructed to rewrite the list using positive synonyms: fearful became prudent; smarty, quickwitted;

clumsy, unskilled; frank, honest; excusing, merciful; foolhardy, adventurous; obstinate, unyielding. "Don't you want your youngster to be unyielding when his faith is challenged?" the professor pushed us. "When he is behaving childishly your job is to see the difference between the definitions. Then you set course to encourage maturing that God-given quality that was placed in him to fulfill his life's destiny."

One way to accomplish this is to always refer to the child with positive descriptors if there is a chance he is within earshot. (Kids believe you are telling the real truth when you think they aren't listening!) Certainly you must teach, train, apply consequences and sometimes punish. Make sure though, that in each situation your words clarify the positive aspects of a trait they've used mistakenly and build up their understanding of it.

"You are to give him the name Jesus, because he will save his people from their sins," the angel instructed Joseph (Matthew 1:21). What do you call your children? To what destiny does that name call them?

CONTENTMENT

One May, many years ago, I had a perfect morning... the kind moms with long To Do lists wistfully dream about enjoying. It began with a colorful sunrise and a warm, light breeze as I took my dawn walk. Returning home, I found the nursling still asleep and Jerry munching cereal, so we had a just-a-couple, midweek breakfast together.

As he left for the office, alarm clocks began to ring awakening the oldest children, but the baby amazingly slept on as did the preschool son. With only two children up, the routine flowed effortlessly; lunches were packed efficiently without the chatterbox three-year-old at my elbow. Uninterrupted, I could help our daughter with a troublesome violin passage. Also, the oldest son who wanted to recite his Bible verse assignment a couple more times before leaving for classes (at the time, we were under the cover of a Christian school where he attended one day each week). We three had time for leisurely talk and prayer before the yellow bus arrived.

Soon pitter-pats sounded down the hall. "Has the bible school started?" worried the middle child who was attending a one-week preschool program with a neighborhood friend. Assured that he had plenty of time, the two of us, as well, had a relaxed meal, music practice, and story before he departed. Finally, the baby awakened after most of my chores were completed. Consequently, we had a play-filled morning without my having to find ways of occupying him so as to get the necessaries accomplished. Even though the remainder of the day was chock-full, that bonus of quality, focused, individual attention seemed to have stoked our emotional tanks so completely that tension just didn't manifest in any of us.

Well, that was then, and that morning was unique. In retrospect, it was actually less fulfilling than other, far more busy, mornings. While it was pleasant, even blissful, it lacked challenge. It's in the pinch and press of daily living that we acquire management skills. For me, more gratification accrues from juggling multiple tasks. The absence of provocation made this morning seem like perfection, but staying the course of routine is a greater accomplishment.

Not long after my perfect morning, Jerry and I were invited to a dinner party where I discovered an exquisite piece of needlework hanging in the powder room of our host's home. It had been created in the mid-1700s by a five -year-old child. In scrupulously even stitches were wrought the words, "Sweet are the thoughts that savor of content; the quiet mind is richer than a crown." It reminded me of Goethe's Nine Requisites for Contented Living, read years earlier in a college literature assignment:

> Health enough to make work a pleasure.
> Wealth enough to support your needs.
> Strength enough to battle with difficulties and over-come them.
> Grace enough to confess your sins and forsake them.
> Patience enough to toil until some good is accom-plished.

Charity enough to see some good in your neighbor.

Love enough to move you to be useful and to be helpful to others.

Faith enough to make real the things of God.

Hope enough to remove all anxious fears concerning the future.

I considered my recent hankering that perfect mornings be constant. Chagrin enveloped me. I'd been tormenting myself by imagining that a phantom mother who has perennially perfect mornings actually exists; a woman with a supportive-cast family straight off of a magazine cover. Succumbing to covetousness, it's easy to become hypnotized in such negative thought patterns. Just enough is, truly, all I really need.

Furthermore, during the child-raising years, whenever I moaned about an aspect of my life, the youngsters began to complain more about their situation, too. Since I modeled grumbling, they believed they too had permission to gripe. We'd all forgotten the peace that accompanies contentment; and the tenth commandment. Looking back, one perfect morning in life is enough.

ANOTHER EDUCATIONAL GOAL

"What would it take to get you to say yes to something, Mom?" a quartet of speculative children asked one busy morning. "You'd all have to grovel before me, kiss my feet, raise your hands in supplication and intone, 'Please, oh beautiful Mother, whom I worship and adore, may I...?'" was my sarcastic response. And they all did! Thereafter the procedure became a humorous rite, although employed only for hugely important requests. When a child knelt, I knew I'd better listen with my heart as well as my ears. If only I could have devised such an attention-getting communication to use on them.

Our first educational goal was, "Learn to manage yourself so you are free to become educated." Teaching it was another matter. From infancy, we applauded every sign of self-sufficiency displayed by the children, even if bedmaking by the eighteen-month-old was a mere attempt to pull up the covers. "You're trying. Thank you." Appropriate acknowledgment of efforts was integral. "You are SOOOOO GOOOOOD! to help Mommy!" patronizes. Helping in the family is fundamental behavior; ordinary jobs get ordinary recognition—a shoulder pat, tousled hair, a smile, or a wink being as or more effective than words. Listening carefully, sitting quietly, waiting patiently, staying on-task, and following through were the major pre-academic skills the little ones practiced and the older children ingrained. When the four- and-five-year-olds wanted to "do school, too" a page of dot-to-dots or drawing paper to make a picture of the story we were reading was doled out *and had to be finished.* "At Hunter Academy, assignments are completed," I'd shrug.

"Why do I hafta?" occurred frequently enough that Mom needed some whine-stopper responses. The kids inevitably heard these words whenever they attempted to weasel: "*Nevertheless*, the paper must be recopied; illegible handwriting is unkind to your reader." "*Regardless*, you must show the math procedure you used." "*Nevertheless*, the toys must be picked up." "*Regardless*, your chore is to empty the trash." After delivery, I'd walk away silently. Though it was tempting to respond to their grumbles, if I dignified murmurs with a reply, the incident mushroomed. Adults have developed the sophistication to mutter in their heads; children haven't. Better to deal with griping as a character issue at a neutral time. I chanted, "*When* you have … *then* you may …" a trillion times, plus another refrain, "Yep, it is hard, but you can *persevere.*"

Consequences instead of threats also produced more responsible behavior. As an example, we licensed trikes and bicycles after evaluating pedaling, braking, and steering skills; defining geographic boundaries, maintenance, and storage criteria. The certificate was signed by both parents and the new driver. A vehicle ridden out of bounds or control, not put away, or mistreated was chained without comment or recrimination. When the (usually) twenty-four-hour sentence had been served, the chain was quietly released. If children wanted the privilege of self-transportation, they had the responsibility of using their equipment properly and wisely. Why the bike was impounded was rarely discussed at the time; offenders reasoned that for themselves with great sighs and self-remonstrations.

Having observed many demonstrations of their parents enforcing the house rules in the practical arenas of life, the kids tended to believe we meant business in the academic world as well. Instead of cajoling classroom laggards, we dispensed minute timers so children might pace themselves. However, when schoolwork was due, it was due—no extensions. Having children home 24/7 is wearing. It's less so if parents make it clear that they will do nothing their youngsters are able to do profitably for themselves.

"Are we there yet?" is backseat litany on family vacations. It's the same in growing children. Remember that they are God's means of completing the growing up of adults. While I found modeling to my offspring was more effective than lecturing, nonetheless, biting my tongue and responding thoughtfully instead of with knee-jerk retaliation were disciplines I'd never have endured just for myself. It's when we come to the end of ourselves that we are open for Him to encourage us and show us more of Himself and His kind of life. "Have I arrived, Lord?" "No, but we're getting there...trust Me."

Daily Life

The Organizational Hamster
Taking Responsibility
Meal Planning
Table Manners
Family Vacations
Extracurricular Activity
Part-Time Jobs
Seasonal Parameters

THE ORGANIZATIONAL HAMSTER

To do and when to do, that is the question. I'm referring to the mental list that most of us have churning in our heads. The more organized have committed that list to paper although ticking off the tasks may not happen according to the anticipated schedule. One theory admonishes getting the toughest, most onerous duties done first. Greater efficiency results when problems don't hang over your head. Another suggests beginning with the easiest stuff so the swell of accomplishment will ride you over the harder things.

There is another theory: if you don't leap too quickly, a job may go away, or get done by some other person who's tired of staring at the mess, or by one who decides to curry favor with Mom by doing it for her. When in a quandary or just pooped, moms may procrastinate. Under such circumstances, it counts as a lesser-known virtue.

The more we nag, threaten, or reward, the less responsible children seem to be. Often, they have never truly experienced the results of their immature approach to life. We need to aim them, but let consequences do most of the talking. Once, when mutiny brewed over the vegetable-to-dessert ratio in the menu, Jerry and I decided to let an object lesson occur. We bought several bucketsful of ice cream in various flavors and when dinnertime arrived, set out a large bowl and spoon for each person. "We decided you kids had a point," we smiled. "Eat as much as you like. Mom's taking a kitchen vacation." The novelty wore off days before the ice cream disappeared. We waited until they pled for real food before granting salads. For a while, afterwards, suggesting, "There's always ice cream," meant plates were cleaned quickly.

When parents give all the directions, children don't develop the interior fiber needed to work on their own—even when they are fully capable. A day came when I had had it with housework and trying to keep ahead of the junk and stuff that got scattered faster than I could scoop it up. Fuming and muttering, I made a poster of every task needed to keep the place functioning. When it was finished, the scope of home management became graphically apparent to all members of the family. No wonder Mom was often frazzled and witchy. Perhaps her assertion that she had little time for fun activities was correct. A group effort divided the work into day-sized, age-sized portions. Rather than spend an entire day slopping mops and fluttering dust cloths, we did a little each morning. Newly reconciled to less than day-to-day spotlessness (which I hadn't been able to maintain anyway), I was secure that at least weekly, all surfaces were disinfected or cleared off. Job reminders weren't given, although another family phrase, "Hamsters, man your wheels!" announced chore-time.

The children, then ages four to fourteen, were intelligent enough to independently decipher instructions for computer games, therefore, manipulative claims of not understanding how to do something that had been explained and demonstrated weren't legitimate. In the new regime, I refused to be suckered into debates or listen to whines. The bathroom, stocked with a book or two, became my haven during those moments.

As the system was implemented, to avoid personal embarrassment, we invited in only understanding friends. It didn't take that long, actually, until the realization sank in that the state of the home place was up to the entire family's cooperative efforts. Then sibling peer pressure followed up. "Hey, my buddies are coming over, man. Why haven't you dumped that stinking litterbox?" How nice to not be the parental heavy.

Nowadays, the household maintenance list remains posted but the chore-children no longer live at home. To do and when to do? "Granny-hamster, onto thy wheel!"

Taking Responsibility

I did something foolish recently, which made a BIG MESS and took forever to clean up. When I told our adult children about my plight, they smiled and looked or sounded sympathetic, but the situation was mine to restore. Embarrassingly, at my "advanced age," I wanted to pout and run away from my predicament.

The error was this: in August, I usually wash the feather pillows I inherited from grandmothers and great aunts. After the worst of the hot sweaty weather passes, I like beginning the fall cleaning with fresh pillows. It's sort of an "at least something's done" encouragement to myself. And washing pillows is not difficult. You begin by picking out a couple inches of seam stitching then reclose the opening with an old diaper pin. Doing this ensures that water pressure doesn't split the ticking yet the feathers stay put. I filled the washing machine with appropriate suds, tossed in two pillows and, as an afterthought, added a dozen items waiting in the delicates basket to fill out the load.

After a few minutes for the machine to begin agitation, I peeked inside to see that everything was submerged and sloshing. Despite my precautions, however, both tickings had burst. Feathers were everywhere, clogging the filter and sticking into all the clothing. It was a preventable incident for, if I had used my wits, I'd have observed that those long-used tickings needed replacing, and, further, I should not have combined apparel and pillows.

Scooping sodden feathers and squeezing out water, I recalled the *Little House* incident when Laura decided to surprise her traveling parents with a top-to-bottom cleaned house. Her enthusiasm outpaced her organizational skills, however, and the task got rather out of hand before completion.

Such good intentions she had! As I had had and as my children had many times during their learning years. Sorting out bedrooms or collections of "really important stuff" and long-term school projects mushroomed for our kids. Predictably, they'd cave in, vault the piles in search of snacks, and then try to slip away from the mountainous mess they'd created.

Teaching divide and conquer, whether a bedroom, an essay, or a project, is an important lesson for educators to communicate. Life rarely affords the luxury of completing a large task in a single session. Building organizing habits takes so much time that it's tempting to command our students instead: "Do this now; that next."

However, an autonomous learner was my goal. Before presenting academic organization concepts, I taught seven- and eight-year-olds how to follow directions by assigning assembly of increasingly complex model airplane kits. They were astonished at the first assignment and gleeful at subsequent ones. Breaking a big job into manageable units was refined by sewing ski bags and simple garments during middle school years.

Growing up, my father's admonition, "Plan! Don't jump on your horse and try to ride off in all directions at once," had fostered confident independence but never quelled my verve. He was careful to verbalize procedures and identify the stages of his projects so we children could anticipate as we observed. "What will come next?" he'd quiz, winking if we were accurate and reexplaining as needed.

After laying a foundation of practical experiences, I segued into demonstrating how to map the scope of an academic project—making appointments for library research, drafting, proofing, and rewriting. Teachers have to guide this procedure many times before children will do so unassisted. A desk pad-sized calendar has enough space to line up a school project, with some color-coding to identify types of tasks and midpoint check-in dates. Part of the evaluation I made of the children's work included their organizational procedure.

Back in the laundry, with no rescuers appearing, I zippered the soggy mass of feathers into pillow protectors and tossed the works into the dryer, remembering to add tennis balls to bump the sacks off the dryer's baffles so they'd tumble and fluff. Then I had to purchase new ticking at the fabric store, sew it up, stuff the feathers in, and sew the opening closed. Then I picked feathers from the garments, including some of my undies. Finally, I vacuumed the laundry area. Still, sitting in a meeting a few days later, I discovered I'd missed one feather, and concentrating on the discussion became challenging. Next year, this student will execute her homework more observantly.

MEAL PLANNING

A plaque hangs in my mother's kitchen.

Wives who cook and do the dishes should be granted these three wishes:
A grateful mate; a well-kissed cheek; and a restaurant dinner once a week.

"What's for dinner?" gives me a headache. Middle-class moms must come up with a variety of tempting meals or risk "Not this again!" complaints. Sometimes I've almost envied Third World mothers whose families are grateful for any nourishment no matter how repetitious. My mother taught me to plan the week's menus then write the grocery list. As a working woman, she didn't have time for nightly market stops to procure missing items. Neither did I. For many years we had only one car; Jerry's dinner would have been late, indeed, if I'd gone collecting ingredients after he crossed the threshold.

Still, the menus, daily activities, and my energy level were often out of synch. Moreover, I got stymied coming up with fresh ideas. Once, to break out of our culinary ruts, a neighbor and I challenged each other to concoct meals by first selecting the vegetable. Another time we began with the salad choice. It gave us mind cramps but we did use up wads of clipped recipes we'd been meaning to try ... what does go with Brussels sprouts????

The daily grind toward 6 P.M. stimulated fervent "Oh help, Lord" arrow prayers—whether I was advance planning or staring into the pantry at 5:15. An epiphany when cleaning out my purse suggested a remedy. Reviewing the accumulated menu and grocery lists, I created from them a twenty-eight-day master that (shhhhh!) was repeated without the family being the wiser. While doing so, I also considered the calendar and assigned specific types of food to certain days according to the activity schedule. Why prepare a time-consuming recipe to be gobbled in eight-and-a-half minutes in order to meet a car pool?

Monday, with laundry followed by Scouts and choral society rehearsal in the evening, I assembled a ground meat casserole dish early in the morning. Tuesday (shopping and errand day) featured chicken, fresh from the butcher with the smelly skin and bones departing in the next day's garbage pickup. Wednesday became our meatless, or nearly so night, inspired by Lenten abstinence. Thursday evenings, inevitably meeting-filled, we guzzled soup.

Weekend dinners incorporated expandable recipes to facilitate hospitality. For several years, Friday was ethnic food night. Each month we explored cuisine from a particular country, also learning some customs plus geography trivia. The Saturday tradition was homemade, whole-wheat-dough pizza. Sunday, we prepared a cut of meat or barbecued. Once devised, the "food calendar" hung inside a cupboard door for reference, yet I wasn't bound to it. If a new recipe turned up, surprise night occurred.

Putting the children in charge of lunches had already been part of our household scheme. Mom was NOT the school cook. Being midday-vittle-prepper was considered a perk because their morning studies ended twenty to thirty minutes early. Unfinished work, however, had to be completed during afternoon study hall, so young cooks usually hustled to prevent academic leftovers.

Some years ago I traveled nationally with speaking engagements a dozen weekends each year. Rather than be frazzled on departure Fridays, I gave the children responsibility for preparing that evening's dinner. They negotiated menu and cooking assignments amongst themselves. On shopping day the quartet paraded the grocery store unsupervised—the preschooler strapped in the cart, a youngster sprawled on the lower rack, an older child pushing, and the fourth checking lists and running the calculator. Sometimes the menu was revised as they spotted new possibilities. "Do we like anchovies?" "Let's get dessert first, then see how much is left for the rest!" Jerry, who had to eat their efforts, also enforced no-second-dinner consequences if the planned repast turned out skimpy. The children's shopping for one meal took as long to accomplish as my whole week's list, but those trips I shopped peacefully unaccompanied and always at least an aisle away.

Nowadays, cross-country trips to assist aging parents occur regularly but I depart without Herculean kitchen labors. The guys take pride in fending for themselves. Once, I returned to find a cartoon prominently displayed that depicted a restaurant scene, the server advising two male patrons about a suddenly revamped menu: "In a surprise corporate raid we've lost our executive chef. However, we proudly offer a good crisis-born businessman's lunch." Bon appetit!

TABLE MANNERS

Our Bible-camp counselor son, home for a few days of R&R, regaled us with tales of life with small boys in the northern woods. "Guess what, Mom," he chuckled, " 'someday' arrived."

"Someday" being that threat frustrated parents utter when especially exasperated, as in "Someday you'll thank me for this..." or "Someday, when you have children..." and "You'll understand, someday."

At camp, a new set of challenges arrives every Sunday afternoon. One brood was woefully lacking in table manners. Neither hints nor admonishments had any noticeable effect. Even allowing for the informality of a summer camp's dining hall, they were, in a word, gross. An e-mail home plaintively inquired, "Mom, do we still have the pig?"

Many years ago, while helping the preschoolers pick up their toys, I spotted the plastic farm set pig and its little pen. Grimly, I confiscated the porker, plunked it onto the center of the dining room table, and made an emergency phone call to Jerry's office. You see, the atmosphere of our family mealtimes had deteriorated into a litany of reprimands regarding where elbows belonged, why chewing mouths are kept closed, and how beverages are supposed to be drunk. I had come to dread dinnertime. Conversation had long ceased. It was essential that the situation change.

At supper that same night, the new rules Jerry and I had fabricated over the telephone were introduced. Henceforth, no unsolicited comments about table manners would be made (the children cheered wildly!). However, if an infraction was detected by anyone, the observer could silently move the pig out of the pen to a spot in front of the offender's plate. If requested, a very short explanation for the pig's arrival had to be courteously delivered: slurping, licking fingers, huge bite of food.

Furthermore, the pig could be sent on to a new home as soon as another lapse was noticed elsewhere. We kept no tally of offenses, but when the meal ended, the pig's final "owner" got to help Mom do the dishes.

The plan worked perfectly. Actually, we parents seldom got our hands on our porcine etiquette assistant. Within a few days the kids had manners reminder signals established among themselves and a strategy developed that stuck Dad with the pig every night. Having read that it takes at least twenty-one continuous days of practice to ingrain a new habit, we let their game continue for over a month. By then the children had internalized the fundamental social graces we'd been so unsuccessful trying to lecture into them.

The pig, we reminded our camp counselor, departed at a garage sale long ago. Amused that he remembered the old ruse, we were glad he'd also recalled that a touch of humor helps a lot in resolving the most annoying situations.

FAMILY VACATIONS

"But you must know about foot-fan chairs," our seven-year-old protested to the National Park Service tour guide who, even with a Master's Degree in American History, had been unable to satisfactorily answer his question. Flustered, the guide maneuvered towards Jerry to inquire how our son knew so much about Benjamin Franklin and his environs. "He's under contract as our Philadelphia expert," was Dad's dry response.

Our family vacations were usually traveling seminars. After determining locale and route, we issued a "call for papers" eight weeks before departure. Because tangible benefit from their academic energies peeked on the short-term horizon, the children willingly read, researched, and wrote in preparation to assuming the role of escort once we'd reached the location of their topic. At the White House, our tour group was very large; the presentation was inaudible to those in the back half. Within a few minutes, the group divided itself with the rear echelon clustered around our fourteen-year-old whose research had included the Presidential home. When the annoyed guide admonished the stragglers to stop lagging, several tourists chided that, "There's a kid back here who's interesting, knows as much as you do, and we can hear him!"

We stimulated assimilation of general information by awarding an "A for the day" if the children's questions received kudos from the professional guides at an attraction. Memory joggers recorded on 3x5 cards were kept in hip pockets ready for instant access. Two weeks later, a foot-fan chair was spotted in George Washington's study at Mount Vernon where the docents were also put through the Hunter Academy question wringer.

Map skills naturally fit with travel. At age eight, the children began to be capable of reading commercial maps so we'd plan a weekend junket to put new skills to use. Elevated on enough pillows to see through the windshield, our navigator supervised the driver who steered as directed (imminent danger situations excepted). When getting the family from home to campsite rests entirely on your shoulders, there's reason to thoroughly learn symbols, key, scale, and compass rose.

For our children, visiting grandparents was never a quick trip across town. Whether to Arizona in winter or Washington in summer, it was thirty-six driving hours, plus fueling, plus restroom searches. Although we never employed this stratagem, an acquaintance kept cross-country calm in his vehicle by dumping one hundred quarters into a travel cup and placing it plus an empty in the car drink holder. "This is extra spending money for you unless I have to settle an altercation, warn about excess noise, or hear a whining voice. Then a quarter transfers to the empty cup and becomes adult spending money. Every hour of silence restores a lost coin." The trip, by all reports, was remarkably peaceful.

En route, my job was anarchy suppression, entertainment, and filling tummies; Jerry never relinquished the wheel. We drove visually boring stretches at night while the back seat slept. Midmorning we'd stop at small town city parks (generally empty, yet meticulously maintained) for a two-hour brunch/play/driver-sleep time. Staple items in the travel kit were soccer balls and glider airplanes to encourage lots of running.

A manila envelope contained clippings and notes of unique sites or twists on the familiar—like visiting the Lincoln Memorial after dark for the emotional impact of the lighting. The perennial suggestions of read aloud books with cliffhanger attributes and ones related to the locale, license plate watching, and round-robin storytelling do work. *Focus on the Family's* directory of Christian radio stations allows favorite programs to travel with you.

When six people settle into a midsized auto, the fit is snug. Each child had a small knapsack to hold entertainment items, jacket, "lovey critter," and the notebook containing their research paper. Zipper pouches punched to fit the 3-ring binder were accommodating carryalls and limited the size of treasures that just had to follow a child home. Souvenirs had to reinforce the learning aspects of our trip. Among them were Scouting patches earned for hiking Bright Angel Trail into the Grand Canyon. From Philadelphia came a scarf with signatures of the Founding Fathers; vials of Mount Saint Helens ash were collected from the devastated landscape. We purchased candlesticks after observing the Jamestown Colony glassblower's demonstration.

Everyone carried a camera. Those under age ten got a disposable until they proved they wouldn't lose it. There was a daily limit on snaps after one child shot an entire roll of his nose before we'd gotten past our city's border. In fairness, children observe things adults don't or they see from a unique angle. Young photographers took some of our favorite pictures.

Bring your funnybones when traveling. On a tight return from Seattle to Minneapolis, we ate at a Wyoming Perkins and spotted clown noses in their wishing well reward box. I begged one for each of us that we wore the whole day, nonchalantly enjoying the startled reactions of passengers in other cars along the interstate. Creating trip-related lyrics to old tunes sped the time, too: "Salmon flopped on the railroad track; fell from the fishmonger's box. Round the bend came the 7:18. Toot, toot! Bagels and lox."

EXTRACURRICULAR ACTIVITY

Granny, finally, went to a prom. In high school I disdained the event as ridiculous, superficial nonsense. Also, I only had eyes for a tall, blond, blue-eyed "Kraut" who didn't go to my school. However, we did attend the same college where I learned to run slowly enough that eventually he got the idea and caught me.

One late spring evening, Jerry and I were chaperones at the annual Senior High Dinner Cruise for home-educated teens throughout the state. The event originated with one of our sons, who declared in September of his senior year that he wasn't graduating without a shindig. He wanted some glamour and romance to mark the conclusion of his youth and childhood. In his next breath, though, he emphasized that he didn't want a rehash of some unpleasant scenes we'd witnessed in our community. "I guess I'll just have to be a pioneer," he mused, "and start the right kind of affair myself."

Throughout time there have been rites of passage—cultural markers—that accorded increasing status to young people. My dad tells about his first pair of long pants at age thirteen; younger boys wore knickers. Sweet sixteen parties and eighth grade graduation were rites of passage until WWII. Our Jewish friends celebrate Bar Mitzvah and Bat Mitzvah. Nowadays, former milestones like driver licensing and high school graduation are so commonplace as to be taken for granted. Less sophisticated cultures have ordeals and rituals. But in twentieth-century America, prom is when the young folks slick on a veneer of adult dress, palate, and activity for a night of magic, fluttering their wings in an imitation of the grownup world. Our exchange students related that they and classmates in their home countries dreamt about American proms. And why not? Toddlers are allowed the privilege of fairy-tale make-believe and old-marrieds reminisce on B&B weekends. Why shouldn't teens have a night to remember?

Some parents worry that dastardly behavior may occur. Others fuss it's frivolous. The excesses of certain party nights are grievous. But we, who have poured so much training into our children, might have courage that the lessons took. At times we can lighten up and let our teens (and ourselves) discover how much maturity they have internalized. The question becomes, "Are they truly virtuous or only so for lack of opportunity to be otherwise?" While the family is still there to nurture and exhort, selected excursions into adult realms are beneficial and fun. Reinstating some of those historic milestones gets my vote, too.

Our son and his group of friends brainstormed all kinds of possibilities for their special evening. Settling on a boat as a unique venue also prevented party crashers and thwarted notions of sneaking off alone. They established dress standards, determined a nonhomeschooled guest policy, wrote a liability waiver, engaged a caterer, enacted music parameters, and mounted a publicity campaign. In seeking chaperones, they included a home-educating father who is a police officer, but no parents of attendees.

"Would you have wanted your parents along on your special night?" was their astonished chorus.

The only planning aspect that required adult assistance was in signing the contracts. No committee member had reached their eighteenth birthday yet. The ship's captain, who had tried unsuccessfully for several years to promote an all-night, after-prom party through local high schools, encouraged them all the way.

So the crew cast off and the old paddlewheel craft plied the lake on a golden evening. The student committee served punch while the catered buffet dinner was laid out. Later there were party bubbles to blow on the top deck, games in the salon, and a little dance music for those who had parental approval. Dessert was served as we glided to the dock where the formal portraits taken at boarding were back from the one-hour photoshop. Just the kind of night any teen (or a Granny) would want to remember.

Part-Time Jobs

It was our German exchange-student daughter who wised us up to a major difference between American teen culture and that of her native Deutschland. Ten days into our year together, she requested a private conversation with Jerry and me to apologize for the financial hardship her presence in our home was "obviously" causing. Her parents, she assured us, would be sending a monthly check for board and room so that our teens could quit their part-time jobs and focus all their energies on their studies.

In the States, after-school employment is assumed to foster initiative, responsibility, and time management as well as bolster a young person's bank account. However, in the rest of the world, while students may work during summer vacations, when school is in session studying is their primary occupation.

Our children, listening to paternal tales of youthful entrepreneurship, dreamed up their own enterprises. Grandma rummaged through her closets and sent the mimeographed flyer Jerry passed around his neighborhood at age thirteen: "I am a responsible kid on your block," which went on to enumerate the tasks he could help busy homeowners with.

Our kids bred hamsters, mowed lawns, minded young children and the pets of vacationers, mucked out gutters, sewed ski hats, and hung holiday lights, thus building initial resumes and acquiring workplace demeanor at an age where mistakes had fewer consequences than they would in a W-2 environment. I had to stifle my overly responsible-mom instincts and leave children to suffer the results of haphazard performance. When an irritated customer called to complain about the length of his grass, as secretary, I only took the message. Comments to either party were verboten.

However, the day came when our adolescents desired "real employment," and we discussed several areas before they went formal job hunting.

First, we talked about their purpose for having a job. Accumulating resources towards financial goals like college tuition, purchasing tools for one's trade, or to make a down payment on a house tops receiving a few shekels to fund hanging out with friends. What general occupational skills would they be learning for future use?

One child, observing the employment history of other teens, declared that, following an early career in lawn mowing, he did not want to advance to either fast food or pushing a grocery cart. After earning the Boy Scout cycling merit badge and familiarizing himself with the manuals of the brands handled at a nearby sport shop, he applied for a position as a "builder"—one who assembles a bike from factory-shipped components. Within a year he was hired away by a local chain as a junior mechanic. Before that summer's end, he was enticed to join the team of a competitor who catered to elite athletes, a position that continued into college.

A second issue we discussed addressed our parameters for potential jobs. Jerry and I thought it was prudent to set these in place before the job search commenced. If academic achievement began to slip, how much leeway did our student have before we required a resignation? We also had some scruples about their clerking amid certain types of merchandise. The matter of working on Sunday had to be pondered. Were they going to be available at all on the Sabbath or only after attending worship services? We insisted they negotiate limits on hours or days or activity before signing a contract.

Next we had to work through how the proceeds from this employment would be used. Allowing unrestricted spending of a paycheck when Mom and Dad still supply food, housing, medical coverage, and clothing establishes fiscal habits and an appetite for fulfilling wants that can't be kept up indefinitely. We passed on the advice of a financial consultant who recommended that, even for teens, a tithe is fundamental. He advised that 50 percent of take-home pay should go into long-term savings or investment. "Reserve 25 percent for short-term goals like driver's education tuition, durable sport and hobby equipment, travel, or a mission's trip," he suggested. The remaining money became discretionary funds but had to cover new financial obligations incurred with maturity, such as a share of car insurance and, of course, all job-related clothing and transportation.

Then there are the practicalities of teen employment to consider. How will commuting to work be handled? Is Mom's car available (and what will that do to her taxi schedule?) or will another vehicle need to be acquired? If so, is your child still working for those original goals or now just to pay for the car?

Lunches on the job need discussion too. What will they cost? If brown bagging is the choice, who makes them or provides the contents? Finally, what flexibility exists for family vacations and significant celebrations? How will you maintain time for family connectedness with another wage earner to plan around?

We found no universal solutions to any of these questions. Talking them through, however, kept channels more clear. We underscored that Mom and Dad were on the teens' side, helping them to cut apron strings and be prepared to meet the world on adult terms.

SEASONAL PARAMETERS

When a newly-wed son brought his wife home for Christmas, a shocking sight greeted him. In the three years since he'd last been home for the holidays, we had succumbed to convenience: an artificial tree stood in the living room.

"I can't believe this," he exclaimed. "All the way home I've been talking about how we always went out on Thanksgiving weekend to cut the tree, the gymnastics we'd go through to wire it to the ceiling rafters so the cats wouldn't bring it down and, especially, how good it smelled because it was freshly cut. Do you still celebrate any of the traditions we used to have?"

This is the son who wrote a lengthy paper at age eleven regarding our family's traditions. (We hadn't realized that we had so many!) However, for him, these "hooks to hang the year on" brought security and a sense of family identity. The Old Testament is full of admonitions to the Israelites to make memorial stones as reminders of events. There are also explicit directions for celebrating festivals at the various seasons. Traditions can be meaningless time- and money-wasters, or they can nurture faith and build human as well as spiritual bonds.

Jerry and I had many discussions to work out the differences in our expectations of holidays. We began with common ground. We were both Christmas-morning-present people, a legacy from our both having parents with five-and-dime stores. Small business owners put in long hours November through December; Christmas Eve is the first night home in over a month. Our folks needed a few hours to get ready for celebrating the following morning. A tradition in my family home was breakfast fixings plus craft materials in our stockings so we children would be entertained while Mom and Dad slept in. Jerry and his brother gift-wrapped all the Christmas packages after their mother had boxed and sealed them. Each was numbered and she kept the code list on her person; they often discovered they'd decorated their own present.

We considered many issues. What expectations did we have about various celebrations? What kind of dollar, physical effort, or time investment had we internalized growing up? Was that what we wanted now? What activities were so emotionally bound into celebrations that we just couldn't drop them? Were there ones we really didn't care deeply about? Which eternal values could be developed in our family through holiday observances?

When chatting with new acquaintances, one of our conversational gambits is to ask about family traditions. It is fascinating to glimpse another family's life through both their innovative and homey practices. Some traditions that we eventually settled upon included homemade pizza on Saturday evenings throughout the year and dessert eaten in 'jammies just before bed every night while Mom read to the family.

Each year, we abandoned the house on October 31 for dinner at a restaurant and organized a simple, but enthusiastic neighborhood parade on Fourth of July morning that ended on our lawn with red, white, and blue Popsicles for all participants. (A library cassette of John Phillips Sousa imparted some musical patriotism.) At the conclusion of our Thanksgiving Dinners, one child recounted the hardships of the Pilgrims while the rest of us, stuffed to the gills, contemplated a serving of five kernels of corn—their ration in the starving time. Would we have felt thankful under such circumstances?

Throughout Advent, we assembled on Sunday evenings for cookies, eggnog, and carols while Jerry read selections from both Scripture and secular writings to tell the never-ending story of God's love for His children. Our brood worked out the logistics of Advent candle lighting by having the youngest child take his turn on the first Sunday when only one candle was involved and working upward through the ranks on subsequent nights. The eldest, therefore the most experienced, handled the matches when all four tapers were set ablaze. We acquired a Lenten cross and similarly marked the six weeks leading to Easter.

And there was that Christmas tree. It took all afternoon to travel to the tree farm, negotiate the decision of which evergreen was most perfect, and picnic in the snow with cider and cocoa to warm us up. What a proud moment when a child grew old enough to handle the saw! An angel touches the ceiling (Jerry's family tradition) and the ornaments are unmatched—many are Christian symbols plus the child-crafted decorations accumulated through the years. Many of them are now missing since a new tradition sends a box of ornaments with newly wed children.

One practice was unbroken all the years the children were at home. In December, school continued as usual. The holiday bustle had to fit around studies or be dropped during this home-education-season of our lives. It seemed to us that "study to show yourself approved unto God" was eternally much more important than decorations or shopping or baking. While there are academically applicable aspects of the seasonal preparations, allowing such activities to encroach upon school abets our children celebrating Saturnalia, not Christ's birth, and encourages idolatry rather than growth in their faith. Interestingly, when we were firm about maintaining academics, the other tasks were accomplished, too.

It requires discipline to insist that traditions serve our purposes, to not let ourselves become slaves to ritual. The best traditions remind us of relationships, growth, beauty, and our place in God's kingdom.

Inner Life

PERSONAL PARAMETERS

Visiting with home-educating parents, our talk some-times turns to children's extracurricular activities. Specifically, the parallel volunteer commitment of parents to facilitate those programs is brought up. Once, while soliciting suggestions to restore balance and sanity, a mother pointed out that when children are in an activity, the parent is virtually obligated to help out. "I don't have anything more to give," she lamented. "It isn't that I mean to shirk responsibility, but I am really getting stretched too thin." Another parent chimed in, observing, "Our children do need an occasional rest from us! Mine appreciate hav-ing someone other than Mom or Dad in charge." Sighed another, "It seems as though we teacher-parents are the primary ones the neighborhood and the community looks to for making things happen."

I have always tried to reserve the month of July as a respite from everything other than family activities. Few phone calls are returned; no home education-related work is permitted. During those four weeks I attempt to recharge my mental batteries with gardening, pleasure reading, and crafts. These pastimes allow for idle musing and latitude to reflect and dream. During July, I never made school decisions nor organized; no formal plans were created. In my lexicon, July and hiatus are synonyms.

One day my mulling turned to those issues raised by the parents quoted above. "You are pressed and pulled," the inner voice said. "Time is the medium that I have given to you for wise investment and despite circumstances, everyone has the same amount of it to spend. When life is finished, the accounting will be according to the fruit produced by your labors; the quality of your witness. Then you will enter into My rest. While you groan at the calendar written black before the month even begins, each activity means another opportunity to share the agape of Jesus. In this fallen world, dependable, cheerful service speaks loudly of Me."

Thus inspiration came. Why wait to be assigned to do something? Why not consider the particular organization's likely needs and, when registering the child, make a preemptive offer of help? An offer, mind you, that took into account the other obligations I'd incurred and my interests and abilities. Too often, I'd been asked to do things that were exactly opposite of my gifting. Those were the years when helping out had been especially draining.

When August and real organizing efforts commenced, I wrote out parameters for myself. First, each child had a limit on number of activities: Scouts, church, a sport, and one fine art. Multiplied by four, that still represented an enormous energy outlay. I dodged teaching Sunday school but contributed in the library instead. After considering the time, effort, and stress of various helping roles, I offered my chosen services early. Thus I was generally assured a mix of major and minor tasks that was parent-sized and balanced for me.

Finally, I learned to smile, say no, and stick to it. "I'd love to have you get to participate in that," I would commiserate with a child, "but Mom just can't add anything more and be a pleasant person." Sometimes they'd chose to call the phone list or bake the cookies or stuff the envelopes—in other words, do my "job," so they could engage in a program. Eventually acceptance grew that superwoman didn't live here; in fact, she never did.

MOM HAS RIGHTS?

My mother warned me that there were things that I'd be giving up, although I thought she meant my career with its perks and satisfying recognition. Nevertheless, waiting out the days to becoming a Mommy was hard. I was impatient to hold and snuggle this wee person who was so close and yet not exactly here. Some decades later, I now know what Mom meant.

Once the baby arrived, I discovered that I'd given up my right to be rested. Also relinquished was the right to have an always tidy house. Baby stuff encroached into every room despite multiple, daily rounds of putting it away. Furthermore, I had innocently handed over my right to a calm and peaceful life. Now I suffered the temptation of fretful thoughts. Was development on schedule? Would I ever again have a moment for myself?

As our little one grew, I found I'd unknowingly surrendered the right to use the bathroom in privacy. The screams of abandonment gave way to steady knocks on the door by the crawler. Knocks gave way to the door being flung open as toddler hands learned to work the knob. Fortunately, once each child developed a sense of personal modesty, this right was returned.

Nor was the food on my plate exclusively mine. No matter that we ate the same menu, snitching from Mom was more fun. Also rescinded was the right to own and display nice things. However, I instigated a small offensive and bought a few unbreakable dust catchers at garage sales so we could practice admiring with a single, gentle finger.

By age six, an insurrection had to be put down or my right to be kissed in public would have been completely forfeited. The negotiated peace stipulated discreet leave-takings with a ratio of more hugs than smooches.

Then we decided to home educate and I found my right to live inconspicuously was gone as well as my antic-ipated right to have time for hobbies while the children were at school.

When their puberty arrived, I no longer had the right to give children my opinion. Instead, I had to earn oppor-tunities through daily efforts involving mutual respect, understanding, and frequent episodes of clamping my tongue firmly between my teeth. Some friends tell me that that they lost the right to be anything except an embar-rassment to their children during the senior high years. The Lord was gracious, however. Our kids gave me tokens of trust and *their opinions* if I got pushy.

Now they are grown. The hard work to keep commu-nication channels open and develop mutual interests dur-ing their childhood and adolescent years is paying off. Magic has happened: grandchildren are arriving and these now adult children of ours are losing their rights.

Meanwhile, I am regaining some rights to make up for those wrested from me through the years. I now have rights like getting to give grandchildren presents just because I want to; hiding with them at bedtime so their moms can't find us and we can read more stories; giggling together about nothing while everyone else groans; conspiring to stomp in mud puddles. Finally, even though the house still isn't too tidy, I am getting to sleep through the night. To everything there is a season.

THE JANUARY PROJECT

Do you wonder if you'll ever have an opportunity to do any of the things that you'd like to do for yourself? For a long time, whenever I couldn't satisfy a yen to go or do because of (1) nursing baby, (2) toddler, (3) home-schooling, (4) budget, I entered it on an Eventually List. Doing so let me feel that my postponed interests would not be completely forgotten and freed me to accept a gap between now and future satisfaction without quite as many pangs of envy . . . directed at my less encumbered friends. The hardest postponements involved fabric, thread, and yarn.

Perhaps needlework is a genetically based passion, as generations of my female relatives have been adept at handiwork. Taught embroidery at age six, I wove my college senior thesis, and if it can be sewn or stitched, I've probably tried to make it. A "fabric-aholic," I purchase souvenirs of cloth on vacations. However, once the children arrived, stitching time evaporated. Although many mental health experts encourage moms to periodically invest an afternoon on some activity that hasn't a practical end, indulging a hobby still brought guilt pangs. The laundry loomed; the vacuum glowered; the weeds grew. Yes, the mending got done, T-shirts and dresses were sewn, but I wondered if I'd ever have some moments to produce what I dreamed of creating.

"By late spring, I'm on the lookout for my January project," the magazine article's author proclaimed.

Reading further, I discovered a soulmate, who, fond of wielding needle and thread but in the throes of preschoolers herself, was short on time to do so. I liked her solution—reserving all spare and scrounged moments during January for a creative undertaking that could be completed within the month. She chose January to avert cabin fever and post-holiday letdown. When month and project were finished, she had the satisfaction of having begun the year with something accomplished.

If you have an Eventually List, perhaps your yearnings can be satisfied sooner than you think. The practical aspects of reserving time blocks were more surmountable than I imagined, especially after I gave myself permission to try. When I bought the new calendar, I inked January Project across the grid of days. Bravado somewhat quivering, I professed that I was booked for the month. When the holiday decorations came down, the house got a thorough cleaning, then, except for bathrooms and the kitchen floor, was virtually ignored until February. By doubling recipes for soups, stews, and casseroles in November and December, then freezing half, I decreased kitchen time later. Some nights we even used paper plates. Since the children were inside the house or inside snowsuits, their clothes didn't get particularly dirty so laundry lessened. A furniture barricade protected my craft area in the family room yet left me available to supervise playtime.

Portable projects accompanied school lessons. Yes, I confess to counting stitches when hearing recitation. "You weren't really listening!" accused the children, but my distraction had benefit when, minus an over-attentive mother full of too many hints or corrections, they struggled a bit but figured out more answers for themselves.

I encourage parents to teach their children (or learn along with them) some form of needlework. European educators believe this fosters hand-eye coordination, perseverance, attention to detail, and aspiration to commendable workmanship. Developing these skills is part of the standard elementary school curriculum for both girls and boys.

The samplers of American colonial days attest to the capabilities of youngsters given instruction and practice. I treasure the clumsy, earnest, first attempts at embroidery, counted cross-stitch, needlepoint, sewing—even tatting— our kids produced, including the boys after they read about professional male athletes who needlepoint and knit and an astronaut who quilts. Your late-blooming academic may be a whiz on Aida cloth or at patchwork and the skills learned there will transfer to the schoolbooks.

What I didn't anticipate was the pride the children would display toward my stitching. Sauntering through the house with playmates, they would casually acknowledge, "Mom's working on her Project." It seemed important to imply that Mom had a life besides just raising them. Surprisingly soon they were self-reliant; stitching moments became available throughout the year and the January Project, per se, disappeared. During its life, though, it taught the whole family something about priorities and caring for Mom so she could nurture them.

QUIET TIME

"Be still and know that I am God."
— Psalms 46:10

Daily quiet time with the Lord: all Christians who desire to grow and mature in Him must engage in this activity. Yet accomplishing it is, too often, elusive. The woman who is home-educating finds herself pulled in many directions and though her intentions are sincere, the exhaustion of many tasks leave the spirit willing but the flesh more weak than she would like. Even those in leadership suffer this dilemma.

At a home-education conference, one woman described her academic year pledge to enjoy early morning fellowship with the Lord each day. The positive effects were obvious after only a few days and she excitedly exhorted her friends to exert the same discipline. Then, the second week of school, she caught the flu. The third week the children had the flu. By the fourth week she was hurriedly catching up laundry and preparing to leave for the conference. Her devotional lay dusty. Sound familiar?

As a busy mother, I collapsed into the arms of an older, mature Christian sister, feeling intense frustration with lack in this area of my life. While she did not excuse me, she did wisely point out that in failing to be perfect, we may guilt ourselves into inactivity. "Which does the Lord really want," she challenged, "a sanctified life or adherence to formalistic practices? In John 5:39 Jesus admonishes the people that 'you search the scriptures diligently thinking that in them you will find life, but the scriptures point to Me!' Perhaps, for now, you cannot manage an extended time each day alone in the Word, but you can still commune with the Author. He will show you how."

"So, how does a random, nonmorning person commune?" I asked the Lord. My next thought recalled a passage from Mary O'Hara's book, *Thunderhead,* in which a teenage son asks what is life all about, anyway? His mother suggests that life is a gymnasium, entered through birth, exited by death, and filled with apparatus (life experiences) on which to build spiritual muscles. These words had pierced my heart when I first read them at age eleven; now they confirmed that inconsistent communing was not indication of permanent moral lapse, but merely undeveloped spiritual physique. As I repented, creative solutions flooded my mind.

Although we allowed little television, *Mr. Rogers' Neighborhood* was permitted the preschoolers. The half-hour broadcast afforded me a midday opportunity for quiet; the older children were admonished that this was Mother's time with the Lord and it was to be respected. Period. A brief interval just before retiring meant the day's final thoughts were not earthbound. A lasting joy is that even today, it is rare for me to awaken without a hymn or scripture playing in my mind. How amazing to experience Psalm 127:2, " ...for He gives blessings to His beloved in sleep."

I took a cue from a friend who wrote a lengthy book while her children were toddlers (she kept the typewriter on the top of the piano and keyed one sentence at a time as thoughts came to her during the course of the day). My solution was to place several Bibles around the house—bathrooms, laundry area, rocking chair, kitchen (in a recipe book holder)—all open to the same passage so reading could be done in snatches then pondered as other tasks were accomplished. When study had been relegated to a confined period, it was tempting to limit meditation to that same slot.

Of course my freedom to attend Bible studies and other classes was limited to nonschool hours or to when Dad could hold down the fort. Yet, after prayer came provision. An evening hermeneutics class was announced at church. I recalled Christian radio programs for which study guides could be ordered as well as audio and videotape series available at the bookstore. These latter resources built bridges with the children. They couldn't avoid hearing the broadcasts so we all discussed the content.

The Lord has a solution for everyone's situation. Therefore, be open to a unique meeting of your special needs. Since we are home educators, if the answer does not resemble a textbook-type model for personal devotions, don't be surprised.

Reaching for Stars

We went car-camping at Gooseberry Falls along the North Shore of Lake Superior one October. The days were Indian summer-warm but the nights were so cold we all snuggled together in the cargo area of our Suburban truck. I awakened about 3 A.M. to a whimpering toddler who'd rolled out of his sleeping bag. Swathing us under an extra blanket, I drew him against me to warm up. We rocked while his shivering subsided. Suddenly he was out of my arms with his nose pressed to the window. "Lyook at all doze stahrs," he whispered. "Can me touch?" An hour quickly passed while our enthralled tot marveled at the beauty of the heavens arrayed so brightly that I, too, almost thought I could pluck a star to hold.

Throughout his childhood, this boy continued to watch the stars. He was the one who set the alarm and shook us awake to view meteor showers from the back-yard. Fascinated by aviation and space exploration, he kept track of when satellites would pass overhead. At Halley's Comet's reappearance in 1985, he plotted loca-tions in the county where we could view it successfully without interference from metro area lights. He reached for stars in other ways as well, and attained Eagle Scout rank by age fifteen.

Years later, as Private von Gohren, U.S. Army, serving on the front line of Operation Desert Storm during the Persian Gulf War, he confided that his lonesomeness was somewhat mitigated by the clarity of the stars in the utterly black desert night. The familiar constellations were present, although, because of the shift in his latitude position, they were placed a bit differently in relation to the horizon.

It's been more than two decades since he and I first pulled up chairs to the kitchen table and bent over books together. Now home education has become a commonly accepted method of providing for children's educational needs, although still not commonly practiced. Yet, more and more families allow themselves this latitude to reach for their starry dreams, as they've discovered that concepts and skills and knowledge don't have to be acquired in a fixed location. But it is still largely uncharted territory. The scary or rough going moments pull us off up-stretching tiptoes and onto our knees. I've no doubt the Lord planned this. He is concerned with ultimate issues. Educational attainments are important but only as they serve to advance His eternal agenda. Each time I'd admit personal bankruptcy in a situation, His grace did prove sufficient.

James 1:2-4 says "Consider it a sheer gift, friends, when tests and challenges come to you from all sides. You know that under pressure, your faith-life is forced out into the open and shows its true colors. So don't try to get out of anything prematurely. Let it do its work so you become mature and well-developed, not deficient in any way." (*The Message*, Eugene Peterson)

I've discovered the bits of latitude I need in my life to keep me balanced. I've come to realize that observing the elements of the natural world is critical to my emotional equilibrium. I brake to view scenic vistas and yell for the family to thrill with me at sunsets. Being unable to scan the heavens on a cloudy evening brings on a vague sense of disorientation. The stars are neither idols nor harbingers of truth. However, they manifest the creative omnipotence of the Truth. Stargazing reestablishes in my mind, soul, and spirit that He is from everlasting to everlasting. No matter the day's trials or triumphs, I agree with Robert Browning, "God's in His heaven; all's right with the world." With a nightly survey of the sky, the truth of Galatians 6:9 is restored in my person. "And let us not lose heart and grow weary and faint in acting nobly and doing right, for in due time and at the appointed season we shall reap if we do not loosen and relax our courage." (Amplified Bible) May you rest secure in all His promises and may your home education adventure be spangled with bright memories.

ABOUT THE AUTHOR

Pam von Gohren is mom to four grown-up children whom she and her husband, Jerry, began teaching themselves in 1977 after experiences in both government and private institutions. A native of Washington State, Pam graduated from the University of Puget Sound with departmental honors. As the promotional home economist for an electrical utility company, she wrote consumer curriculum for schools and customers. After retiring to become a mother, she organized parent education classes at the newly established neighborhood health house for children in the Hilltop area of Tacoma. Following a move to the Midwest, Pam became the North Central USA regional administrator for La Leche League International, helped start a private school and with Jerry, served on the board of directors for the Minnesota Association of Christian

Home Educators. She is a certified trainer for Parenting for Achievement classes. At present, Pam serves on the Minnesota Nonpublic Education Council, a body created by statute to advise the Commissioner of Education on private school matters.

Besides conducting workshops and seminars, Pam has spoken at the annual conferences of Minnesota Association of Christian Home Educators, North Dakota Home School Association, and Home-Based Educators Accrediting Association, as well as the national conferences of Home School Legal Defense Association, La Leche League International and Marriage Encounter. For information regarding speaking engagements, visit the web site of Learning at Home Successfully: http://www.isd.net/home-ed-pro.